The Collapse of Wo

The Collapse of Work

CLIVE JENKINS
& BARRIE SHERMAN

Eyre Methuen

First published 1979
by Eyre Methuen Ltd
11 New Fetter Lane, London EC4P 4EE

© 1979 Clive Jenkins & Barrie Sherman

Set, printed and bound in Great Britain by
Cox & Wyman Ltd,
London, Fakenham and Reading

ISBN 0 413 45750 8 (hardback)
      0 413 45760 5 (paperback)

Contents

Acknowledgments

The authors would like to make it abundantly clear that this book could not have been written without the help of many other individuals, and research papers. The subject is in essence so new and so fraught with different interpretations that this sort of help was both inevitable and also very welcome. Whilst it is always traditional to suggest that it is invidious to select certain people or pieces of work it is also traditional to ignore this particular caution. For probably the only time in this book we shall conform to tradition.

We would like to thank the Research Department at the Association of Scientific, Technical and Managerial Staffs and in particular Peter Bennett, Peter Bowyer and Campbell Matheson whose help was invaluable; our thanks are also due to Tim Webb A.S.T.M.S. who read the book and made helpful comments. We would also like to thank Ray Curnow of Sussex University, both for his verbal contributions and for the information that he and the Science Policy Research Unit of Sussex University provided. We thank our secretaries Rose Apter and Greta Karpin for their forbearance and aid and finally thank all those people with whom we have shared platforms, meetings and conferences, for their advice and ideas even if only to discard them.

Clive Jenkins
Barrie Sherman

Preface

The number of people registered as unemployed in the United Kingdom has been hovering around the 1½ million mark for some 3 years and has not fallen below a million since the summer of 1975. This figure, however, is almost certainly an underestimate, as many commentators now believe that unemployment is actually over 2 million. In itself this is a disturbing situation. But what makes it even more alarming is the combination of the increasing length of time people are remaining jobless and the fact that at least 300,000 young people have been temporarily removed from the statistics by the use of various short-term measures. Regrettably it is a common habit in the U.K. to treat the high unemployment and other unpleasant phenomena as peculiarly British, and to simplify the unemployment debate to a ridiculous extent by introducing emotive words such as 'scroungers'.

Nothing can be further from the truth. Unemployment is now a truly international problem and the armies of jobless people are digging in all over the industrialized world. Well over 6 million are unemployed in the Common Market countries alone, and that figure does not include 'guest workers' who have returned to their own countries. In the U.S.A., Canada, Italy, Belgium and Austria, for example, the unemployment rate is considerably in excess of that of the U.K., and both Germany and France have over a million unemployed.

Two disparate economic forces have created this international problem. The first is the short-term world trade recession – although in truth it has been continuing over a very long period. The second is the changes in industrial structure and the more efficient use of both people and machinery to produce an increasingly slower growing volume of goods and services.

These high levels of unemployment have all developed without the aid of any major changes in technology. But we now stand on the threshold, indeed are just passing beyond that, of a new industrial revolution, based on developments in micro-electronics. It will have the most profound effect on jobs and employment prospects since the introduction of the electric motor and before that of the steam engine, because as with those two previous breakthroughs no production process will be immune from its impact. Indeed it may even be more potent since it will affect not only processes and components but also commercial activities, and office, clerical and information methods in both the public and private sectors of the economy. This quantum leap in technology will accelerate the structural changes in the pattern of employment which have been steadily advancing over the past decade and will exert an immensely destructive impact on both existing jobs and the future supply of work.

Unemployment, which has been synonymous with slumps and low investment will, for the next few decades, be equally the product of high investment and booms.

To date there has been little in-depth discussion of structural or technological unemployment. This book is intended to fill this gap and to stimulate such a debate. It not only examines the new technological breakthroughs, the reasons why they are occurring, and where and how their impacts will be most directly felt, but also analyses the present economic climate and the nature of work itself.

No longer is it good enough to repeat the old clichés and slogans about work and unemployment any more than it is sufficient to rely upon the traditional short-term palliatives. We shall have to fundamentally question why we work, how we take our leisure, and whether work itself is a positive activity. This must be done not only in the context of the United Kingdom but internationally too, both to determine these activities in individual countries and also to establish the basis for international action.

It is not enough, however, to sit back and debate abstract propositions. Action is required and required soon by

governments, by employers, by trade unions, by educational-
ists and by society in general. Some of these actions will have to
be radical when viewed against traditional political and social
responses but historically so were those that followed in the
wake of the first two industrial revolutions. The whole process
may well be painful, but what is certain is that to sit back and
wait for the tidal waves of technological unemployment to
engulf the international communities will be infinitely worse.

This book is dedicated to preventive actions rather than
drastic cures.

London   *December, 1978*

1 The technology/work dilemma

Any person who worked during the first industrial revolution would not recognize, indeed would not believe the world as it is today. Not only would the motor car, the aeroplane, the telephone, broadcasting, and even kitchen equipment totally bewilder him, but even the workplace with its new machinery and organization would be alien. For that matter people who were living and working in the 1930s, if transported to the present, would be almost as surprised. The pace of change, especially technological change, has been growing at an ever-increasing rate; new products and developments in existing and new products now follow upon one another with startling rapidity. The computer press recently published a heartfelt plea from computer users to slow down on the new developments so that existing systems can be stabilized and used to their full potential rather than having to be emended every few months.

Yet the past 10 years have seen a slow-down in fundamental changes. Many of the new products merely offer stylistic or other small changes to existing products, as in the motor vehicle and pharmaceutical industries, and whilst some new technologies have taken root, for example colour television, supersonic flight, numerically controlled machine tools and computers, these are the exceptions. Major technological breakthroughs are rare; ones which change the fundamental nature of society rarer still. Most of them are highly visible and impinge on the consumer or the onlooker, but not all, for there are those which are used in work processes or in components which go to make up a whole machine. Both functions have repercussions on the way we work and the amount of work available.

Work, like technology, is a staple commodity in modern industrialized societies and is firmly inter-related with technology. Technological developments can create work, can destroy work, and nearly always change work whether by altering the product or service or, indeed, the work process itself. This imposes major strains on workers because as techniques change so skills, often laboriously acquired, become obsolete and in turn the consequent retraining exacerbates the stress on the various branches of our education system. Yet, whether skills become outdated or not, whether people start to feel inadequate at work or not, they do feel that they *have* to work – and not only for the money. The work ethic is so deeply ingrained in British and other industrialized societies that work has acquired a value in itself, even though it is widely regarded as unpleasant.

Each ordinary weekday morning roughly 18 million people leave their beds and then their homes to go to work. At the same time $11\frac{1}{2}$ million children and students of varying ages go through the same routine to learn and acquire the necessary knowledge and skills to *enable* them to go to work. Until now only the retired, the sick and disabled, housewives and some shift workers avoid this exodus. But there is a new group that is excluded, a group that is growing and that this book suggests will enlarge further – the unemployed.

This movement to the place of work results in the rush-hour. Roads are jammed by vehicles designed for four passengers but carrying only one driver. Buses, trains and the underground systems are full; queues develop and lengthen, tempers fray and few kindly words, indeed few words are spoken. That same evening the process will be repeated. Whatever the weather, whatever the counter-attractions and however much people dislike the work itself, this process repeats itself – it has its own dynamic.

Few people welcome getting out of bed in the morning; fewer have ever claimed to enjoy the journey to work, and few admit to enjoying their jobs; yet at present nearly all would fight to retain these disadvantages. This is the great paradox. By and large people do not enjoy their jobs, yet they have to work to earn the money upon which they and their families depend. This is the economist's view of work – a non-pleasurable activity which attracts a monetary compensation.

Yet even if this compensation is not paid there is a considerable amount of evidence that work is still needed. If religion was the opium of the masses then work is the castor-oil of the population.

Given this over-riding need, it is somewhat surprising to find that the one activity that neither the United Kingdom, nor indeed other Western economies have been able to provide is a constant supply of work or access to it for all. Whilst this has been achieved for short periods, circumstances have tended to dictate that these are followed by periods of less than full employment. At the time of the first industrial revolution and indeed up to the outbreak of the Second World War this state of affairs was in some senses acceptable. Expectations were low both in material goods and in political demands and responses. But this has now changed; expectations are high and rising, and at present worklessness inevitably means exclusion from this chain of expectations: in other words, past high levels of unemployment will no longer be tolerated with the equanimity and forebearance that history might suggest.

The technology in existence at any given moment in time clearly must have a great impact on the type and amount of work available. It determines the types of products and services and the methods by which they are made, packaged and distributed, and society is firmly based on the acquisition of products. These range through food, housing and clothing to consumer durables, holidays, health services, education and hairdo's – with both the private and public sectors involved in the process. Most technological changes have been applied directly to the goods or services and have directly stimulated the availability and production of new ones. This has enabled economies to expand and provide employment at one and the same time. However, we are now standing on the threshold of a new breakthrough which, at present, acts primarily on the process side alone.

Micro-electronics or microprocessors or semi-conductor technologies are not new in themselves, but in a developmental commercial sense they are. The ability of the devices incorporating this new technology actually to perform their functions, and perform them well, is no longer in question any more than is the fact that they are capable of the widest of applications. As the first report of the Advisory Council for Applied Research and Development ('The Applications of Semi-Conductor Technology', September 1978) put it: 'This is the most influential technology of the twentieth century because: (i) it both extends and displaces a wide range of intellectual or intuitive skills; (ii) it is all pervasive; (iii) it is still advancing rapidly; (iv) it is very cheap and getting cheaper; (v) it will become abundantly available from international sources and (vi) it has exceptional reliability.' The Prime Minister stated it more simply at the December 1978 meeting of the National Economic Development Office when he described micro-electronics as 'the most rapid industrial change in history'.

It is, however, a technology the main attribute of which increases productivity rather than stimulating the production of new goods and services. It is this aspect, benevolent in all respects save the need to work, upon which this book concentrates. For if productivity rises dramatically, as indeed it will, then given the same, or even a higher level of demand for goods and services, employment will fall and work prospects will diminish. This is the essential dilemma – it is clearly in nearly everyone's interests to adopt these new techniques, yet by so doing the probability is that the industrialized world will find itself faced with the growing spectre of unemployment.

This matter was one of great interest to the Trades Union Congress in Brighton in 1978. In his Presidential Address David Basnett said: 'This new technology will mean a loss of jobs at least as massive as the first technological revolution meant, and that poses our members and therefore this movement with problems.' He also pointed out that 'by 1985 in the E.E.C there will be a net nine million more entrants on the labour market seeking jobs. At the same time a combination of technology and the world economic recession will be destroying jobs faster than they are created.' At the same Congress the Prime Minister referred to the importance of microprocessors but concentrated only on the production of them by the new National Enterprise Board-INMOS partnership and the efforts being made by the Department of Industry to make British managements aware of the new possibilities. This emphasis was both laudable and understandable. However, he did not even

4

speculate that there *might* be an employment problem as a result.

A month later at the Labour Party Conference in Blackpool the Prime Minister expanded his view: 'Tomorrow's employment will depend on our response to unprecedented technical change; a rate of change that is ever more rapid. And we must move fast to catch up. To take an example, the microprocessor is beginning to make many of our long-established mechanical processes hopelessly out of date – *thousands of tasks both simple and complicated will disappear*' (our emphasis). If thousands of tasks disappear then so will millions of jobs, on the simple assumption that each task has on average at least 1000 people performing it. However, having, somewhat obliquely, raised the subject the Prime Minister went on to play it down. 'A Government that turned its back on these developments would impoverish its people. Labour will instead harness them to produce cheaper and better products, generate extra demand and thereby build extra jobs.' This praiseworthy statement conceals a host of political, economic and social difficulties, especially in its conclusion, the creation of extra jobs. Is it that easy or indeed possible? Is it necessary or should we rather start to change our attitudes to work as the technological revolution sweeps on? In essence the argument is the old one – do we work to live or live to work? The question is serious and demands a serious debate. Whilst society *had* to have people working to provide all of its goods and services the question was esoteric, but the new technologies will change this context. People will be disemployed, and yet the goods and services still will be provided. One can postulate that the volume of goods and services should be increased, thereby creating more work. This is indeed one option, but it must be realized that on the one hand it would require a radical change in income distribution to enable those who at present cannot purchase to do so, and on the other, that given the nature of the technology few new jobs would be created. It is in the labour intensive industries that jobs can be created and, typically, these are in the public sector areas, health, education and social services.

It cannot be denied that there exist real needs in these areas and these must become part of any future policy not only to provide jobs but also a better life for all. Yet at the same time we

5

must ask ourselves what is so special about work and is it arranged properly over an individual's lifetime? Is it not ludicrous to slave away week after week, year after year and only have a large block of leisure at precisely the time when we need it least and can use it the least – at retirement? We need to spend time with our growing families, not have the time when families have dispersed; we need to recover from the steady energy attrition of concentrated work yet rarely get the opportunity except in small breaks. What is so special about work, especially if it will no longer be so necessary, that we make such a fetish of it?

The Haiitians have a very wise and perceptive old proverb 'If work were a good thing the rich would have found a way of keeping it all to themselves'. This does not appear to be an argument that endears itself to the majority of people in industrialized countries, although perhaps it deserves to be taken more seriously.

Despite the payment of unemployment benefits and other social security payments, and despite a basically free health service which removes one great fear of having little money, work is still sought after. Relative poverty has by and large replaced absolute poverty. As Josiah Wedgwood found in his famous studies, the basis of poverty changes as peoples' expectations change, and expectations have risen. Indeed they have rocketed, deliberately stimulated in order to sustain growing consumer based economies. Yet despite these underpinnings (and taking account of the relative poverty) work is still something to be fought for.

'The right to work' remains a powerful and emotive slogan, even if, in a capitalist society, it must be meaningless. It is powerful enough to bring in its wake marches, demonstrations and confrontations. The Upper Clyde Shipbuilders' work-in, turning strike action on its head, and scores of other less publicized and less successful imitations, were also born partly out of the desire to work rather than merely to earn. One has only to read the speeches of the leaders of these actions to realize that they knew they were striking a popular chord.

What of the obverse side of the coin? Again nothing has changed. Despite the fact that currently Britain has 1·5 million unemployed (2·1 million using O.E.C.D. standardized data)

6

and the E.E.C. countries have 6·5 million out of work, certain politicians still use the term 'scroungers' to describe the unemployed, especially if they have the temerity to claim their due under the United Kingdom Social Security provisions. Not only is it all their own fault but they have politically obnoxious claims to want to live like others in society.

Of course life is not as simplistic as this at all. Some people are looking for work, others are ready to stop and take early retirement. Some people feel the need to work, yet the self same people may vote with their feet and take a 3-day weekend. It is all part of this schizophrenic approach to work – people need it but frequently dislike it. We believe that the time has come to treat the schizophrenia. In other words we would like to postulate a leisure revolution. In our view the prime impulse to bring this about is technological change, although it is by no means the only factor.

Technological change has always promised much and delivered less. The world is littered with the debris of past breakthroughs; whatever happened to the 'Bacon Cell' which promised to revolutionize transport, or 'Zeta' as the new miracle energy source? In addition the fruits of viable breakthroughs often get dissipated. Others prove to be of limited importance, while some have staggering implications, such as steam power, internal combustion and electric motors, all of which have changed societies radically. Communications via telephones, radio, television and new satellites have had immense social repercussions and dangerous behaviour control propensities. Other technologies such as nuclear power, or the linear motor may never fulfil their potential for one reason or another.

Technology does not always work in the interests of people. Weapons research, from napalm to the cruise missile, from I.C.B.M.s to neutron bombs cannot be alleged to have improved the human condition. We now also have the ability to make D.N.A. and to engineer genetically, whilst millions starve in the Sahel, Bangladesh and Latin America. The distribution of technological change and the financial returns to it are obviously skewed. This need not be the case, it is merely that we have *allowed it* to develop in this way.

Clearly no new technological breakthrough is entirely

predictable at the outset either as to its success or its development. The microprocessor is no different. It is probable that it has enormous potential but it is not certain that this will be fulfilled. It is equally probable that it will stimulate a new technological, indeed industrial revolution, yet again it is not certain; however, by definition, probabilities are more likely to occur than possibilities. This book is premised on the fact that the new technologies will be used, although it is quite easy to see some areas where they would not be allowed to reach their full potential.

If technological change is to have a beneficial effect it must achieve the maximum good for the maximum number of people. On past experience this does not occur automatically, requiring instead a series of political decisions to ensure the required effect. Some breakthroughs such as the train, car, bus, or plane, stimulated a large change in social behaviour and few would disagree that this has proved beneficial. Mobility gives widened physical horizons and blurs the margins of social structures, and both consequences have resulted from these breakthroughs. However, as with all changes there are costs as well as benefits. Motorway and airport building are both environmentally damaging and contentious and the car itself claims 20,000 victims per year on the highways of the world – more than malaria and morphine addiction added together. No doubt the new technologies will suffer from similar disadvantages, although at this stage it is difficult to see quite what the direct social costs will be.

The indirect social costs, the changes which will occur to and within workforces, in industrialized, semi-industrialized and developing economies are basically predictable. Fewer jobs will be needed to produce the same level of goods and services, and there must be very radical changes in job content, in training schemes and in the resulting strains on social structure systems.

The microprocessor is thus capable of changing productive and commercial processes and of challenging the existing political and social mores. In all respects it is a powerful tool. It is not too fanciful to compare it with the steam engine or, even more fundamentally, with the wheel in its impact. The wheel certainly stimulated employment and social advance, and yet it also necessitated restrictive legislation such as driving on one side of the road and speed limits. This type of trade-off is precisely what this book argues for. Yet some technological changes are able to alter the balance between work and leisure by replacing, in part, human labour, whereas others can alter and enhance leisure activities themselves. Machine tools are an example of the former, and television and cinematography of the latter. Microprocessors have the ability to do both.

Economists have always believed that employees work until their monetary reward is sufficient and then they trade off work for leisure. What needs stressing for this context and for many others throughout this book is that when reference is made to 'work' it is to paid employment. In theory of course this is wrong. Housewives work, but are not employed; hobbies are work, but are non-paid. In fact work can be a form of leisure – anyone who has had to dig over flower beds or weed a vegetable patch will testify to the work element. Equally 'leisure' in this book refers to periods when people are not actually taking part in paid employment, whether or not they are 'working' in their leisure time. In taking this view we are merely reflecting most people's perception of work and leisure; amateur gardeners never actually refer to their efforts as work, any more than do hobbyists such as potters or stamp collectors.

Leisure and leisure activities are the obverse side of the work coin. Few people have the choice that economists discuss, that of stopping work to take leisure when they feel they have enough money. Generally speaking only the self-employed professionals such as dentists, solicitors and accountants enjoy this luxury. For the average industrial worker there are fixed hours tied to the process on which he or she is working, as is the case for administrative or clerical staffs. Others have jobs where quite simply the work has to be done and these include doctors, managers and trade union officials. Broadly, in these circumstances, the difficulty is to find any time for leisure.

Not only do people in Britain react in widely different ways when confronted with periods of time-off, but the inter-country responses are also very different. One argument against leisure *per se* is that people would get bored quickly, preferring to be at work. We find this a morally dubious argument, for people have never been educated to use leisure periods and in any event work conditions have ensured that they are unused to them. A

9

shift in the ethos of society towards leisure and away from work would, we believe, trail behind itself a change of attitude. In any case the boredom argument often reflects an assumption of boredom by those making the very judgement in the first place, an assumption which is subjectively based on their own version of what constitutes non-boring activity. As those who pontificate on this matter are most often highly literate or verbal and equally middle class too, they transmit their prejudices. Listening to Vivaldi has a higher value than relaxing over the racing page; reading Kafka is less boring than lying in bed – this is the message. Some people actively like to lie abed, like to chat in their local and like to sit and fish, watch television or play football with their children. They are not bored, nor, in their own selves do they feel that their time is being used unproductively. The use of leisure must be left to those who have it.

There is no doubt, however, that our education system has signally failed to provide people with enough knowledge to make their own choices concerning leisure activities. It has seen its function in a totally different light. But in the same way that the higher levels of education widen peoples' job options, leisure should be one main factor in both the primary and secondary systems. Education, both conventional and life-long, will have a great part to play in the future, but there will have to be a re-appraisal of its overall role.

This book is entitled *The Collapse of Work* and by this we mean that industrialized societies will not, in the future, be able to provide work for all on a *continuing basis*. Although the book largely will be about Britain and British institutions, the problems will repeat themselves in all developed economies whilst other and new problems will occur within the less-developed economies. Although this may appear to be disastrous, both the international dimension and the nature of the technological changes together hold out the prospect of great opportunities; rather than being the result of a failure of demand it will be the greater efficiency of supply that will prove to be the engine of the changes. It follows that the problems and thus the remedies are basically those of the medium term. The possibilities for great social advance will exist. But it must also be recognized that the possibilities of a backward step towards a 'post-industrial dark age' exist too.

It is work, or the lack of it, people's attitude to it and the changes that will occur in the types available, that will be the fundamental point from which political and economic action will stem. But this in itself conceals a host of fundamental questions. What do we want of life? Does this differ as between nations? If so, can the differences be reconciled? Is life about consumption of consumer durables, about power, about enjoying oneself, about reproducing the species, or about political freedom? Is it a combination of these and if so how are they weighted and what other factors interplay with them? If there is a possibility of change then these sorts of questions have to be broached; more than anything else a revolution in attitudes is in prospect.

Previous technological changes stimulated both debate as to their desirability and the direst of predictions, especially those concerning employment, but these were never fulfilled, especially those in our recent past. Our argument will be that what has happened in the past will not necessarily be the pattern for the future, and that it is highly unlikely that it will be repeated without overt and positive political action. The argument that technical change did not fulfil the worst predictions is tantamount to saying that because oil has not run out in the past it never will. We hope to show that this new quantum leap in technology will be like no other this century and that, despite the prevailing wisdom, previous major technical changes did bring in their wake radical and often very unpleasant effects especially in employment terms.

Expectations have never been higher in industrialized countries, both in terms of government services (which require government revenue) and personal services and goods. Young people are conditioned by the education system to think of learning in terms of jobs, in terms of income and thereby in terms of consumption. Older people have already been so conditioned. Whereas in the 1930s expectations were, at their highest, for a non-leaky roof, a disease-free life, adequate food (especially for children), steady work and, for a minority, a car, a radio set and smart furniture, these have now altered radically. The 1950s heralded the consumer society of the 'You've Never Had It So Good' era. Intensive advertising, especially through television, wider communications and the 1960s

11

Beatles' concept of working-class based folk heroes have raised people's horizons. Whilst in convenience terms conditions have improved, and whilst there is now a safety net to prevent absolute poverty and rampant disease (although some still slip through), there is a negative side. People have more to lose. More people own houses and have to maintain mortgage payments; more purchase cars, furniture, washing machines or fridges through some form of hire purchase arrangement. A collapse of work would prevent a large number of these people meeting their financial obligations as well as cutting off a large number of young people from what is now regarded as their right, a high and rising standard of living.

Conceivably a society could be run in this way – but it would have to be at bayonet point. It is inconceivable that many societies could simultaneously and permanently be run in this way for the pressures of disaffection would be far too great. Unfortunately, it is equally improbable that any one nation in isolation could take effective and long-lasting steps to solve the unemployment problems that arise. The international dimension of trade and the linkages of transnational companies make a long term successful course of unilateral actions unlikely in both economic and political terms. Comparative disadvantages, once confined to nationally based companies, are now compounded and magnified by the ability of the multination companies to mobilize and transfer immense amounts of finance and resources at prices and in ways which they themselves determine. The world is not like the 1930s in any respect.

A very famous economist (Vassily Leontiev, the refiner if not the inventor of input–output analysis) summed up this present phenomenon in the following, slightly amended way. That the microprocessor will replace human beings at work he has no doubt and it puts him in mind of when the motor car replaced the horse – it was great for human beings but not too good for horses! He might have added that horses did not have the vote.

It is not only the material and political expectations that have changed. Women are entering the labour force in greater numbers than ever before and, more significantly, are rightly expecting equality of treatment. If work collapses at the very time that womens' employment expectations rise, there could be a revival of Lysistrata, at the very least. The same logic applies to the current movements to equality for certain minority groupings in various countries. Neither of these phenomena were previously present and will themselves reinforce any consequences of change. Finally, the *structure* of the labour force has changed in Britain, in Europe and in the U.S.A. More people are employed in 'non-productive' activities; in routine clerical and administrative positions, in services (public and private), and in managerial occupations. Such people will almost certainly be the most vulnerable to the probable changes.

There are, however, other implications of the microprocessor revolution which, over the longer term, societies will have to confront and then learn to adapt to accordingly. Discriminations, not only sexual, but against minorities whether on the basis of colour, religion, race or politics are often at their most violent when economic circumstances are the most unfavourable and in the shorter term the seeds for such bigotry will be falling on promising ground. The relationship between the developed and less-developed countries will change and although even the direction of this change is open to question the new work processes will generate defensive reactions on both sides, and here too we must be alert to avoid North/South confrontations.

If a new technology makes more efficient and simple productive and other processes, there is a chance that we shall use up physical resources more quickly than anticipated even though in the interim the opposite will appear to be true. The early 1970s arguments around the Club of Rome/M.I.T. projections on resource depletion have never been challenged on the fundamental statement that the world's resources are finite. Research into alternate technology and alternate materials must thus proceed with even more urgency. Attitudes to consumption will have to change as radically as attitudes to work. Our present complacency towards investment and finance in general will have to be re-examined and the existing political institutions will themselves have to respond at the pace that the social changes force them to do, rather than at their own more generally leisurely rate.

If governments, unions and employers take the right decisions in short and long terms the 'collapse of work' may be referred to in historical terms as the 'ascent to leisure'. But for this to happen there must be taken a series of difficult decisions which will both fly in the face of established political practice and need international courage and vision. We are not, it must be emphasized, talking of the distant future. For the most part the technologies are known, the developments are being made and the applications marketed. We know only too well the scale of unemployment world-wide and the destabilization that it can bring. It is useless to hold out the chimera of well-being to a society whose younger elements are increasingly cut off from the reality of expectations.

The time scale for change is no more than 5 years long. If this book does nothing but stimulate an informed public discussion of the matter, it will have served its major purpose, providing that those in power act on the results of the debate.

2 Work and technical change

Work is a serious subject. It has rarely been the topic of humorous treatment, and only infrequently has it been used as the main theme in any serious works of art, and then by radical writers pointing to the unpleasantness and inequities involved in the systems providing the work. Only two major exceptions stand out. The film *Modern Times* in which Charlie Chaplin brilliantly juxtaposed the advance of technology and work, and the early efforts of the socialist countries, using posters and drama, to dignify and exhort people to work in the newly changed circumstances. Work is there rather like the air we breathe and take for granted; it is undramatic, certainly not funny, and yet is an inbuilt part of life.

This state of affairs has arisen over time, and appears to have accelerated since the first industrial revolution when continuous working became so important to the establishment.

Nowadays, sociologists claim that people need work to guarantee a complete identity, while others argue that work imparts individual dignity. Certainly those who find themselves out of work would agree in varying degrees with both of these propositions. Whether these reactions indicate that man must work or whether society has imposed work upon him is the key question. Put another way, is the work ethic, or Protestant ethic, a totally natural response?

Nearly all the animal kingdom, especially the sub-division of mammals, who can adapt to different environments, do just enough work to enable them to live. They hunt, singly or in groups, exercise, maintain hygiene and at times play – the idea of work or hunting for its own sake rarely exists, although some stockpile against lack of success or for hibernation. It is probable that early man was similar. The difference of course is that the society of most animals, though complex, is constrained by the physical limitations of the absence of tools, speech and writing. These are all essential for control systems. Almost all human societies, whatever the political system, have had ruling élites which were able by one means or another to get others to work for them. In turn this reinforced the wealth, power and status of the élite itself.

It is thus not surprising that for hundreds of years work has been declared to be 'a good thing'. From the pulpit, the government chamber, the judges' bench, the king's palace, the lord of the manor's house and the factory owner's office, the message has been repeated *ad nauseam*: 'work is good for you and your soul'. From the Middle Ages onwards religion told us that God ordained that the station of most men was to work, and work became associated with such key words as honest, sober, trustworthy. Those who did not work on the other hand, were by implication dishonest, shifty, and drunken.

The concept of work slowly became the paramount motivating force for the individual's own salvation. Society was built upon the premise that everyone should work and those who were unfortunate enough not to find a job were found useful occupations in workhouses. In these institutions the latter were not only forced to do hard, unpleasant work such as oakum stripping but, most importantly for the system, were made to feel both guilty and grateful: guilty, because they had failed themselves in not finding a job, and grateful to the workhouse trustees for providing it for them.

People have two fundamental needs: to live and to reproduce. For this food and an ability to maintain a constant body temperature are essential and this implies a need to obtain clothing and shelter. It is to this end that work is aimed and anything beyond is a luxury in excess of survival. Obviously agriculture, requiring organization and discipline, becomes the first industry because hunting, apart from being unpredictable as a supply of food, was not based on an industrial pattern. Communities, then specialization by a division of labour within them, soon sprang up. The house builders, tool makers, food preparers, clothes makers, and then often landowners and farm labourers were soon differentiated. As villages grew into cities and cities into states, so the complexity of life demanded newer and more diverse skills. From the Renaissance there emerged engineers and architects, potters and jewellery makers, shopkeepers and shoe repairers, tradesmen, clerks, scribes, lawyers, teachers, all specialized in their ways and who charged for their services. Slaves, often taken in imperial conquest, were also trained to carry out sophisticated skills. Interestingly enough, recent evidence suggests that it would have been far more economical to use free men rather than slaves for these tasks.

Artisans employed apprentices and other employees. Small businesses became larger; at least large enough to, albeit infrequently, dominate small markets. Slaves and freemen occasionally worked side by side but, outside of the cities, farming was still family and slave based. As happened over and over in successive countries it was the transition to urban life which made specialization a necessity and consequently stimulated the growth of the working classes.

Obviously different nations developed different work-systems and at differing speeds. The Chinese and Asian systems were based on usurious landlords lending at interest rates which enslaved the peasant population, whilst the cities developed on very similar lines to those in the West. The Turkish and Ottoman countries grew on a slave basis within an agrarian and armed citadel framework. Each of the countries, however, moved from a barter to a money system, and it is this that enables the notion of employment, as opposed to work, to become viable. Both internal and external trade was considerable, leading to the employment of increasing numbers of people. There was, of course, no shortage of labour, since imperial conquests extended territories and the labour force, and the agrarian based population, were, in all, a source of extremely cheap labour. In some countries of the world, of course, this latter situation still prevails. Although the less-developed countries are the obvious examples, France, Spain, Portugal and Greece are all countries where the transfer of labour from the agricultural sector to the industrial sector would not be at the expense of any significant productivity.

Although the Dark Ages in Europe wiped out most of the trappings of Roman civilization and tribal warfare became the rule, both work and trade continued. Feudalism, long and well entrenched in Asia established itself in the West, whilst the very slow development of merchants, traders and artisans continued in the cities. Work for the majority continued to be for survival. For many centuries this was to be the history of the West. Plagues and famines due to crop failures and wars took their toll of people on the land and after a short period forced families into the towns. The churches and monasteries provided the education such as it was and also acted as landlords and employers. Interestingly, the formal teaching system – almost for the last time up to the present day – was geared to learning as a good thing in itself, rather than either directly vocational or as a preparation for working life.

As trade increased in importance, so merchants and ports, towns and cities grew, with the services on which these depended. Agriculture was still the basic work, but more and more small entrepreneurial enterprises – for example, cotton, mining, iron and steel smelting, clothing and building – sprang up. With the development of alternative methods of using power the size of the small factories grew. Wind and water were the two major sources of energy but both dictated the site of the enterprise and thus limited development. Distribution of goods was difficult. Roads were rough (and often unrepaired since the Roman occupation in Britain) and both personal and goods movement had to be made by ox or horse, carts and carriages. As a result each area had to be self-sufficient to a large extent in many of the basic goods – specialization in industrial processes, though present in some measure, came later. However, despite this 'self sufficiency', when a crop failed, as it did roughly one year in ten, starvation and disease struck deeply; it was still an agriculturally based society.

It can well be argued that the greatest technological break-through in history was the development of the wheel and axle. But these early days of work did throw up major inventions and developments. Crop rotation, harrows, techniques capable of cathedral building, gunpowder, the manufacture and the uses of metals and alloys, all ultimately enhanced life and life styles. None of these, however, had applications wide enough, given the other existing technologies, to promote wholesale changes or disruptions in society. The canal system represented a turning point, for the development of canals meant that goods could be transported in bulk; now all that had to be done was to produce them in bulk.

The steam engine, fixed and with huge beams and gearings, changed first Britain and then the world. Machines in mines, in mills, in steelworks, in steel and wood working, indeed in all the productive processes, could and did work harder, faster and more reliably than men. Factories grew up around the engine. For the first time it was possible to have many hundreds of people working in one building purely for the reason that such a method was more productive. The industrial revolution had begun.

From this point onwards there was not only a flowering of talent and ingenuity (previously restricted to the arts and natural sciences, but now applied to engineering and production concepts), but also an urgent need to get labour. The new machines might well have been a step advance over the cottage-style equipment, but they required labour. Each machine needed tending, each machine needed maintenance and each factory needed very many indirect production workers: carriers, sweepers, folders, stackers. Employers were not exactly fussy about who they employed providing their workers produced the goods by the end of the day. Women, children and men, old, worn-out and discarded at 40, were fodder to the growing and hungry plants. The emphasis was on women and children as they were paid even less than the men.

Ill-educated, often first generation from the land, and living in squalid conditions, these people had to work to live. Yet the housing of this period was for its time certainly better than the comparable accommodation provided some 50 years later when industrial production was in full swing. The unfamiliar environment and poor living conditions led to some protestations and early defensive reactions. The political system was such that ordinary working people were totally disenfranchised and the prevailing moral ethos, adumbrated by the church, writers and parliament, was that their opinions could be discounted.

Before the agricultural workers moved into the towns, their work had been regulated by the seasons and by the physical demands of farm animals, and in addition there was some chance that they might obtain food on a home-grown rather than monetary purchase basis. Urban living changed this entirely. A total dependency on wages was the effect of the change and the home worker had to fit into the productive process as defined by the entrepreneur. Equally, whereas in agriculture the weather often thwarted the best work and intentions of all concerned, no such excuse could be made in a factory. Success or failure was controlled by men and work became the most important element; thus, hand in hand with the need to work came the propaganda dignifying work and the working man. In truth, work conditions were so unpleasant and so arduous and dangerous that appeals of this kind to moral and divine truths had to be made to avert the possibility of either mass absenteeism or even a revolution.

Most employment needed neither literacy nor numeracy; the skills and crafts that either survived or were indeed created, were passed on by example. Clerical staff were few, administrative staffs fewer still and a managerial cadre (outside of owners) almost non-existent.

There was thus little need for a system of mass education and consolation, and recreation outside of work was mainly provided by the Church. The large and ornate churches still standing amidst mean streets bear witness to this conscious effort. Partly this was a pious effort by the Church to save souls, but it was also the opportunity not only to preach the work ethic but also to provide a spiritual regeneration for the coming 6 days. It was, as we have said, important to get workers resigned to their lot. It was on this sort of society, with gin and beer to remove the physical pain, and the Church to remove the spiritual unrest, that our present prosperity was based.

The late eighteenth and early nineteenth centuries saw the growth of towns and cities and uniquely rapid changes in life style. The cultural shock of moving away from the land and agriculture was reinforced by the disciplines imposed by the new types of work. The new technologies and production methods were outstripping the ordinary person's ability to comprehend them or to adjust. The Combination Acts and the ability of justices to impose penalties of appalling severity for trivial crimes checked working people from organizing collectively and at the same time transformed them into an oppressed majority. It was a period of the most immense social upheaval.

Some argue that technology has never created unemployment nor produced anything but good effects. This suggests that there has always been a smooth continuum within which technological changes emerged, replaced or augmented the traditional technologies and no one was hurt or damaged in the process. The first industrial revolution certainly did not follow this Utopian pattern. The social dislocations created many small, often fragmented, opposition movements both within Britain and abroad, when their industrialization arrived. In this respect technology is definitely not neutral.

Two main opponents of the new industrial system were the Luddites and the Chartists. The one focused its fears on to the potential impact of the new technology and the other, more radical, on the state of working and political conditions after the introduction of the new technology in Britain. Luddism was said to be named after Ned Ludd, a stockinger's apprentice from Leicester. He gave his name to the movement, some 20 years later, which believed that machines would de-skill employment. The movement was far from co-ordinated and some machine wrecking was done for 'bargaining purposes' and some for personal revenge. The Luddites' views are often misconstrued as being opposed to the new techniques, mainly in cotton and other textile mills, on the grounds that unemployment would rise. This is only partially true. Their main argument was that the traditional skills would not be needed and whilst they realized that other jobs would be available, they saw only too clearly that these would be less attractive and require less expertise. In short, they were a defensive and to some extent a conservative movement. But they also believed in direct action. If words could not stop machines, sledgehammers could and did. It was a short-lived but bitter movement.

The People's Charter and the Chartist agitators moved within a social maelstrom of violence and unrest in Britain, in France and in the Independence-minded America. When viewed against the post-Marxist revolutionary movements the Charter was mild in its demands, but its drafters' concerns were rooted in the discontent in the new cities with work and with working conditions. Whilst victims of the industrial revolution, they did not want the technologies abandoned or amended. The

Chartists were primarily more interested in changes in the political rather than the industrial structure. The movement, however, lost momentum and fizzled out in the late 1840s and 1850s. This whole period was violent. The Peterloo Massacre and other violent and repressive measures were mirrored by the assassination of the Prime Minister, Spencer Perceval. Repression and bloody riots were one cause of the collapse of Chartism; the first Reform Act was another.

Those who claim that technology has never produced such side-effects as these and then suggest this will always be the case are basing their argument on a false premise. It is quite clear then throughout Britain from the 1760s onwards and originating in the new industrial areas in the east and west Midlands, Yorkshire and central Lancashire, there was an immense social upheaval. Transient labour became permanently employed, dissatisfactions grew, and although the change was sudden and the reforms slow, there *was* reform. Britain was first to the industrial revolution. When it came to other European countries they too had social upheavals and revolution. The Paris Commune and the European 1848 revolutions are evidence of this.

The industrial revolution not only changed the method of production and distribution, but also altered people's awareness of their own problems. Where once religion could claim that a crop failure or a shipwreck were God's retribution for something or another, the Church had to find new reasons for failure. It did so in terms of work and its inherent goodness. Poverty (next to cleanliness) was the preferred state and poverty through work was something most workers knew all about. Whilst the industrial revolution saw a dramatic growth in Britain's national product it was not a smooth economic transition. Adam Smith, the new high priest of economics, believed in the hidden hand guiding his market economy. As with earthquakes and other natural disasters, the hidden hand often seems to develop a tremor. Trade cycles now took over the role of crop failures. Over-production followed by under-production; shortages of labour followed by unemployment all existed with the background of a large reservoir of labour on the land – and especially so after the repeal of the Corn Laws. These short trade cycles have been a feature of market economies ever since. The 3, 5, 7 year cycles are amplified in Britain due to its unique industrial and commercial structure. They are neither mysterious nor divine; they stem from an inability to control either the demand or supply sides of the economy and, in particular, the inability to respond quickly enough to their changes so that full employment equilibrium is a matter of luck rather than economic judgement.

Over this long period of, for the time, rapid change, there were many people prophesying doom and gloom with each succeeding adaptation of technology. These prognostications varied widely. The steam engine and its trains were variously thought to cause heart attacks if they travelled over 20 miles an hour, or cause cows in adjacent fields to miscarry their calves. World-wide revolution was predicted by some as a result of capitalist industrialization, whilst Malthus saw the world drowning under people as incomes rose. Those who foresaw the ending of traditions were correct, but often these traditions were indefensible in anyone's language and new 'traditions', often equally unpalatable, took their place. Although the de-skilling of jobs and trades did occur, new skills sprang up in their place. Indeed, over this entire period few people saw technological change as a threat to the overall number of jobs. Victorian England revelled in technological change. The side effects of it, the slums, the misery, the pollution, the prostitution and the overall poverty and low life expectancy were swept under the moralistic carpet by the expanding middle class. It was this class that was firmly entrenched in government. Some people were aware – Disraeli recognized the 'Two Nations' and laid the political foundation for modern capitalist societies – but overall only a handful of revolutionaries, the emerging trade unions who knew the conditions only too well, and the social reformers publicly cared.

Technology and ingenuity were celebrated no matter who was hurt in the process. Karl Marx certainly saw the seeds of destruction within capitalism; of necessity his scenario demanded technological advance, but his doctrine was the exploitation of the workers involved. He did, however, postulate as part of this exploitation the 'industrial reserve army' which resulted from the industrialization process.

By the turn of the century the cities were established and

23

urban life a fixed and long-standing reality all over Europe. Political development, however, was still slow and this is a crucial point. What was inflicted then in the name of progress and technology on the ordinary people would not be tolerated today. Both the formal political system with its wide franchise, and the development of political awareness in general, would make it very difficult for any democratic system to inflict the degree of economic misery which was taken for granted throughout the nineteenth century in the modern 'civilized world'.

The end of the century saw two more technological breakthroughs – the development of the internal combustion engine and the motor vehicle, and the creation of the electric motor. Both had major impacts on work and society and themselves stimulated other technical breakthroughs, as had the steam engine, some apparently totally unrelated to the primary breakthroughs. In general such major changes appear to exert a catalytic effect, and although some of this can be attributed to the actual new techniques, others are only explicable in the sense of a 'friendly environment' encouraging development.

In its early years the development of motor transport reached nothing like its full potential. But that was reached quite quickly with the development of mass production and the consequential price reductions as these applied both to private cars and the mass transport buses and coaches. The development of mass production also changed working patterns and conditions. Work became even more intense and more repetitious, and the environment with its noise and large area even more hostile. Crafts and skills disappeared at a faster rate than ever before. Service engineering became a growth trade and the component supply industries and companies a growth sector – even down to the Malayan and Latin American rubber tree plantations.

The new productive processes also changed work patterns. The high capital outlay and the need to keep costs to a minimum meant that plant had to be used for 24 hours in a day. The shift system, although already adopted in some areas, was developed or expanded and became the norm. In turn this reduced the quality of working and social life, and stress-related diseases such as stomach ulcers appeared to be associated with shift-working. However, and inexorably, the system expanded in the areas where shift-working was appropriate.

The electric motor probably had more impact on work, production processes and productivity than the steam engine and far outweighs the motor car in its total impact on society. It is small, efficient, capable of adaptation to an extent not thought of in the steam age, and it forms the basis of almost all factory plants, machine tools and modern clerical equipment. It is the prerequisite for most of the existing domestic appliances and is so prevalent that it is taken for granted. The number of jobs created far outweighed those lost in the switch from other forms of power.

Over this entire period from 1890–1918 the world economy was expanding, markets in the industrialized and newly industrializing countries were opening up, whilst the countries with colonies used them as outlets for manufactured goods in return for cheap raw materials and food.

This state of affairs could clearly only continue for as long as the existing income distributions allowed, both nationally and internationally. By the middle 1920s the 'great depression' years had started and, once again, work with its possibility of providing the wherewithal to buy the essential things in life and maintain families was in short supply.

The internal combustion engine and the electric motor created what many people call the second industrial revolution. The de-skilling of jobs and the decline of crafts continued. Work itself became partially more acceptable and less unpleasant (although more repetitious) thanks mainly to trade union actions centred in the United Kingdom and the United States of America. High unemployment was endemic. Keynesian economics was a heresy challenging the classic market view and Marxist experiments were safely isolated in the Soviet Union. Those out of work looked for work because they had to. No work, no food, no house – how was a person to bring up a family in such conditions? Even so, amidst the overwhelming economic reasons for wanting to work there was the underlying philosophy that one *needed* to work. Unemployed people were called 'work-shy' and the response to hunger, the soup kitchens, were based on the familiar pattern of paternalism similar to the 'benevolent' attitudes British administrators adopted towards similar 'unfortunate natives' in the Empire.

Rearmament and war ended the depression. For the third time women entered the labour force in manual occupations and work took on a new meaning. 'Dig for Victory' was paralleled by 'Work for Freedom'. The war actually saw the gestation period of two fundamental pieces of legislation, both of which have an important bearing on our current attitudes to work: first came the Beveridge Report on Social Security matters and then R. A. Butler's 1944 Education Act.

The Second World War changed many attitudes. The notion of women working took a far deeper root than it had after the First World War. Political attitudes changed. After all the Communists had been among the Allies and became, for a time, almost respectable as the governments in Europe fell to the Left. People made it abundantly clear that they had not fought in a major war to return to the low living standards and high unemployment of the 1930s. Enough men and women survived to remember the earlier slogan 'a Land fit for Heroes' – and the actual results. They voted to prohibit a repetition of that misery. As a consequence both the 1945 and 1951 Labour Governments and the 1952 Conservative Government were totally pledged to full employment policies; in the U.S.A., Congress had just failed through a loss of nerve to have the Right to Full Employment written as an amendment into its most hallowed document *The Constitution*. After 1945 Western Europe was rebuilt mainly through Marshall Aid payments from the U.S.A. These enabled governments actually to implement their policies of full employment.

In Britain, although there were hiccoughs, it did appear through the 1950s and early 1960s that full employment was here to stay. Keynesian heresy had become Treasury orthodoxy and Anthony Crosland wrote his famous analysis of Social Democracy based on this short post-war experience. But this book will argue that this period was an aberration, a product of external finance, post-war rebuilding and the Cold War, and that we are now reverting to form.

In addition there was an explosion in the commercial exploitation of the technologies developed during the war years. These ranged across new methods and techniques of production to dramatic pharmaceuticals and new products such as radar, the jet engine, telecommunication developments and all the artificial fibres. It was an unprecedented period for Western Europe, a conjunction of all the most favourable of circumstances, and as a result it appeared that work could be provided in all circumstances.

Real incomes rose together with expectations. These were fulfilled in large measure not only by relatively full employment and more consumer goods but also by political action which changed the social scene.

The education system expanded to provide for universal literacy and numeracy, and implementation of the Robbins Report on higher education more than doubled the number of places at universities, polytechnics and technical colleges. The welfare state introduced by a Labour Government, thus implementing the Beveridge Report, provided an underpinning for society. The elderly could get pensions, the disabled and disadvantaged allowances, and the unemployed some income. Finally, the National Health Service with its treatment free at time of application removed a major anxiety for many families. All these factors played a part in British attitudes to unemployment, and relative impoverishment and a loss of self-respect replaced malnutrition and sickness as the main results of a loss of work. In latter years unemployment has been accepted far more readily than might have been anticipated. The demand for radical change, so common in the 1930s, was most unfashionable in the 1950s and 1960s and seems likely not to be argued into the 1980s, although the new technological developments may change this.

Equally the labour force itself has changed. In Britain there has been a continuous switch from work in manufacturing industry into the service sector, both private and public. This has unfortunately not been associated with increases in output in the manufacturing sector – indeed, it has proved to be the reverse as shown lucidly by Eltis and Bacon of Oxford University in a series of studies and articles. This change could have far-reaching implications when new technologies are considered. Finally, as far as work is concerned, expectations have risen for people expect to work and to a greater extent than ever before expect enjoyable work. These changes are quite natural and quite heartening. There are, however, the small storm-clouds due to short-term economic trends which tend to put a blight on even these modest expectations. The present high levels of unemployment are blamed on one of those storm-clouds, but is this in fact true or is there another explanation?

There is a theory, long forgotten, but now the object of some academic interest, which is named after its propounder, Kondratieff. It is about *long-term* economic waves rather than the short-term, and can be specifically related to technological change, or, to be more precise, major technological changes. It must, however, be admitted that he himself did not attribute the cycles to technology *per se*, but rather he blamed the capitalist system of investment and stock replacement. Also, many changes are not major. The spinning jenny, whilst important in its field and creating many changes in its industry, was confined to that field alone – its effects could be boxed off from the rest of the economy. The steam engine was, however, totally different. It represented, once it had had its 'software' of gears and drives to give a circular motion, the first machine to be produced which was in effect a reliable energy source. Despite its bulk and relatively high capital cost it was involved in nearly all industrial and manufacturing processes for nearly 100 years. It also revolutionized personal transport and the distribution of goods. Canals, once the spur to mechanization, proved to have a mere butterfly usefulness – the steam locomotive was far more efficient. The Kondratieff long waves, lasting from 50 to 75 years, have been noted three times and some economists believe that we are now in the second phase (or indeed the third phase) of a fourth one. As it is so long-term one feature of this theory is that you do not really realize that you are in it. The long-term cycle subsumes many short-term cycles, rather like the graph of an ice age where the ascending or descending curve is not smooth but contains periods of relatively warmer or colder weather of around 100 years. We can just discern the turning points of the short-term cycles but the long-term bear no relation to our consciousness. We can only see the effects with the benefit of hindsight.

Each of the three waves so far has been associated with a great leap in productivity and leaps of these magnitudes must be associated with quantum leaps in technology. The first and second waves concern us at this moment. The first was from 1780 to 1840 and the second from 1840 to 1890. The first was clearly associated with the steam engine and the consequent industrial revolution, the second with the development of the railway system and the electric motor.

These long-term waves can be divided into four cycles. The first is an increase in productivity and volume of output in the economy. This is followed by a period of levelling off on to a plateau followed by a prolonged depression. The final phase is rising output and national product. Thus, whilst long-term benefits accrued in both the cases in question, there were the major slumps and very high unemployment through 1790 onwards and 1870 onwards both lasting for around 25 years and also the great depression of the 1920s/30s.

Whilst this theory is superficially plausible, it may not be correct. More importantly it may tell us nothing of importance when dealing with the future. On the other hand, it may be correct and be of the greatest relevance over the next 50 years or so.

There would appear to be some basic truths. The sharing of the growth in the 'national cake' over the 110 years after the first industrial revolution was very inequitable. Admittedly purchasing power rose for all, but far more so for a few. Equally it cannot be said that despite the growth the standard of living had improved more than marginally for the majority of people. There were indeed two major depressions with mass unemployment and starvation both of long duration and both (by definition) meaning that demand was less than the available supply. Finally, it was also true that there was in both instances a lengthy period of growing income and stability which increased purchasing power. The period up to the late 1920s exhibited many of these same characteristics although the Great War blurred them. For the moment we shall leave this theory suspended and return to it later. Whilst our predictions for the future do not depend on it being an immutable law, it is interesting to see how the third wave and finally the future, fit into Kondratieff's scheme. The theory has been refined by Schumpeter, probably the only modern economist to treat technological change seriously, but is still far from universally accepted.

Work and the nature of work have changed over the centuries; the need for it and the drive to obtain it have not – the Turkish, Yugoslav and Greek 'guest workers' are evidence of this. This book looks at the probability that modern societies will not be able to provide enough work, if present day policies and attitudes prevail, and despite the present passive nature of the unemployed, this lack of work will be destabilizing. This is the cataclysmic approach.

We do not, however, look at the future with the jaundiced eyes of pessimism, rather we think that new horizons could be opened up for workers in all countries – developed and developing. Optimism must be the prevailing mood for the future. Too many generations of humans around the world have sacrificed themselves or been sacrificed to the false ethic of work for reforms not to be attempted. If we fear at all, it has been aptly summed up by Disraeli in *Coningsby*: 'Conservatism discards Prescription, shrinks from Principle, disavows Progress; having rejected all respect for antiquity, it offers no redress for the present and makes no preparation for the future.' A conservative approach to emerging problems will be a disaster – it is the time for political and social imagination to match the technical innovation.

3 The conventional wisdoms?

Contrary to what its proponents have argued, technological change has not advanced with a calm inevitability and a minimum of social disharmony. On the contrary it has brought about not only social and physical misery, and long-term and large-scale unemployment, but it has also stimulated opposition. And yet there are still those who believe that none of this ever happened and argue that it could not happen in the future; while others admit that it did take place but claim that it will not happen again, mainly on the grounds that all such problems can be solved by Keynesian economics and policies. Based as it is on a false premise, that it never happened, the first contention can only be rejected out of hand. The second, however, needs examination, as does the employment impact of technologies introduced this century and, in particular, the much abused computer.

The rate of change of technical progress has increased over the past 200 years. From the 1780s to the 1870s there were many peripheral technical breakthroughs, but no major innovations. There were technical improvements and a plethora of inventions but none structurally changed the nature of *demand* for goods. Industry relied upon its ability to use and adapt steam power, and the traditional industries, built up in the early part of the nineteenth century, dominated. Product innovation was limited and the 'workshop of the world' traded in the tried and tested products on which it had based its reputation. The watershed came in the great depression lasting from 1873 to 1896, and by the end of this period new technologies were being employed. Apart from motor transport and the electric motor discussed previously, the chemical industry started to expand rapidly, especially in Germany, office machinery was developed and large-scale shipbuilding programmes took shape, many of which developments were fuelled by the armaments industry, and the emerging militarism. From this point onwards there was a considerable amount of product and service innovation: electric and gas lighting, cooking, sanitation improvements, the automotive industry and its supplies, radios and clothing all competed to expand. Consumer durables became available to some of the workers for the first time.

The conventional economic wisdom in the industrialized countries was still based on Adam Smith as refined by Marshall and also the 'marginalists'. In running an economy the money supply and its rate of circulation was the main policy measure, budgets had to be balanced and the notion of government spending to compensate for a shortfall in demand was unheard of. Indeed government spending itself and government revenues were both very low. Income tax was not introduced until 1799 and by 1914 had only reached 5p in the pound. Markets, although realized to be imperfect, were assumed to work effectively in a perfect way and the management of the economy was conducted with due deference to this 'hidden hand'. In turn this meant that the booms and slumps in the economy were mainly left to take their own course and when technological change enabled the supply of goods to be increased, the demand side of the economy was left to its own devices; hopefully in time to match the new situation.

Government did not intervene in business, at least not directly. Certainly the repeal of the Corn Laws was a surrender to the business interests represented by the Manchester School and the measure considerably aided British manufacturing industry; imperial acquisitions were unashamedly for commercial reasons. 'Laissez faire', however, remained the order of the day extending to international commerce and the consequent lack of tariffs with the result that Britain developed into a low wage, low cost economy. The new industries sucked people off the land, so that purchasing power in the economy thus increased with each person who moved into the cities – those on the land had been earning so little that even the low industrial wages raised the aggregate. This meant that there was an expanding domestic market to supplement that growing overseas, created by the expansion of the empire.

There was thus a situation where investment and growth forged ahead over the long term, whilst within this movement there were cycles of severe depression and unemployment. Nevertheless, the ability of the economy to keep growing and, at times, provide full employment was in part due to the increased purchasing power of new workers and of the existing workforce. Markets were not saturated and international competition certainly not severe.

The latest of the recurrent 'great depressions' emerged in the 1930s. Although Keynes had formulated his theories and President Roosevelt half-heartedly attempted to put them into practice in the New Deal the 'bankers' solutions' were the favoured ones. Cuts in wages, cuts in public expenditure, very high unemployment and good housekeeping were the policies. Keynesians would argue that their policies could have reversed this situation and effectively reduced unemployment.

Since the Second World War Keynesian style policies have been the rule in Western Europe as a whole and Britain in particular. Despite this there have been periods of quite high unemployment and low output exemplified in the depressions of 1957-8, 1967-9 and 1975-8. It is in this latter period that the rate of increase of technological change increased so rapidly.

The staple industries remain, particularly steel, vehicles, shipbuilding, textiles, mining and chemicals, but some have greatly diminished in importance, whilst others have been modified by technical developments. Yet at the same time whole new industries have sprung up, including television and its component industries, synthetic fibres, plastics and other products, air transport, electronics, telecommunications, drugs and organic chemicals. In the productive infrastructure there has been the development of computers, lasers, nuclear power, control systems, natural gas, chemical engineering and now the new micro-electronics.

Clearly there are two distinct types of innovation. On the one hand totally new products and processes, and on the other products and processes which replace the goods, services or mechanisms already existing. Of course this distinction is occasionally blurred, as in the case of the motor car: it mainly replaced horse-drawn vehicles, but created such new demand that it can be thought of as a new product although for an old use. In turn the economic impact varies according to these two types of innovation. A totally new process, product, or service will have a greater positive effect on growth and employment consequences than a replacement technology. One assumes that replacement is undertaken because of higher efficiency, productivity or profits and in these circumstances there is generally either no change in the number of jobs available or even a diminution.

The inter-war and then post-war years up to the end of the 1960s saw a combination of both types of innovation in products and services. Thus aggregate consumption could rise overall since the mix was primarily slanted to new product and material development, and as markets became saturated so built-in obsolescence became the new order. The periods when the economy slowed down, primarily owing to balance of payments difficulties, were those of higher unemployment, and if the slack in the economy was needed to be taken up public expenditure was increased. This Keynesian demand management approach should have controlled the economy to the extent that there was either full employment (probably with some degree of inflation) or unemployment and lower inflation. Yet it has not done so, and today we find ourselves in a situation of both high unemployment and inflation – the new 'stagflation'.

Keynesians argue for a similar approach to technology. If technology releases resources by enabling goods to be made more cheaply then, they claim, these resources can be mobilized to provide more employment, especially for those made unemployed by the technology. Yet this course of action has to rely upon certain assumptions, some of which are not consistent with the facts of the real world. It assumes a closed economy with no leakages of profits or surpluses. It assumes a mobility of labour and a training system capable of infinite flexibility. It assumes that technological change is smooth and consistent and not 'all embracing'. Finally it assumes that the present system of ownership of the production and service processes would allow the implementation of the policy. The balance of probabilities is that these assumptions are false and that a full employment equilibrium will not be attainable.

It is not only the assumptions that can be seriously questioned in this scenario; the entire economic philosophy as to whether spin-off effects or additional economic benefits arise, is in this instance open to doubt. These benefits appear because the extra income generated is used to supply and purchase goods and services and thus the general level of economic activity rises. Whilst this is true within a limited framework of change there are considerable difficulties when the changes are very widespread.

As this new technology affects most sectors more or less at the same time periods, jobs will be lost across the economy at the same time. This means that to have extra consumer purchasing power the increases in salaries of those working must be at least as much as the salaries lost (net of unemployment pay) through people not working. Thus to have the spin-off benefits appear at all, salary increases over and above normal bargaining increases will be required. However, as those still working will be in the higher salary brackets (and these will become relatively higher) and typically these sort of people save a higher proportion of their income, the consumer effect will be automatically dampened.

On the profit side of the equation the prognosis is equally gloomy. Profits can be used for reinvestment but this in turn is likely to create more job loss. Distributed profits will, in by far the largest measure, go to financial institutions who constitute the largest shareholding bloc. Financial institutions consume little in goods and services and their prudential considerations trap them into 'safe' investment practices involving gilt-edged and blue-chip securities and property purchases. None of these will create beneficial effects in the private sector, especially the service sector. There should, however, be some additional economic benefits, notably through increased exports and import substitution, through the capital goods industry and through the funding of the government debt in the gilt market. However the loss of the basic purchasing effect will mean a far lower spin-off benefit than is being anticipated in some quarters.

The conventional wisdom in Britain at present is that investment has been too low and that productivity needs improving. Invest more, improve productivity and we will create employment – so goes the argument coming from the major political parties. Yet it is clearly the choice and type of investment that will determine the primary number of jobs created and whether or not these are balanced (or overbalanced) by redundancies. Further, the more capital intensive the process the more the rate of return declines (in general terms this is a world wide problem) and thus investment could slow down. The response to the latter could well be to hold down wages, a most unpalatable course of action for trade unionists to contemplate and almost certainly unrealistic in the long term.

It is, however, the assumption that technologies come along when they are needed and for the purposes for which they are needed, together with the even more radical assumption that all technological developments must have the same impact on employment, that is the most unrealistic of assumptions about technological changes. There is always a time gap between the initial invention, its development and its applications. The microprocessor is now in its initial application stage: we know it exists, we know it works, we know it can be applied and we know, from all the available evidence, that its net effect is to reduce employment. In this respect it is totally different from other recent technological developments. However, if the economy is slowing down contemporaneously with a period of rapid technological change, then given the present U.K. position, even Keynesians must admit that the time taken for adjustment to the new system has to be lengthened and unemployment becomes almost inevitable.

The computer is a good case in point of the more traditional technological development. It was a product which stimulated the most appalling predictions of job losses and it trailed unpleasant myths through the incomprehensibility of its processes and jargon. Yet by and large it did not have the results that were predicted, although there were significant and sometimes even severe job changes.

The computer was a new product. Its development and its application were very fast and were often undertaken by enterprises which lacked both the minimum of planning and the minimum of knowledge. It was a physically large apparatus needing space, specially adapted rooms and a large number of staff, both working directly with the machine and also supplying it with information and servicing. The computer was also relatively inflexible. New techniques and processes needed new peripherals and software and these were expensive, especially as the user was nearly always dependent on the original producer to meet his needs. It was and still is accepted that the 'plugs' of a main computer can only work with the 'plugs' of the same producer's software.

In the early days the pattern of computer usage followed a consistently uncritical path. Companies heard that other companies had them or were getting them and felt that they had to keep up. Computers became a status symbol as did the fountains at head offices in the 1950s. Once an installation was purchased there was frequently no board level control and the strategic and tactical planning was left to the newly hired data-processing managers. Two things stemmed from this abdication of control. The first was that cost control was minimal and the systems that had to be set up in order to allow the computer to function at all were not thought through. The second was that it was always in the interest of the data processing (D.P.) manager to build up the department in personnel terms (as it is in so many organizations), and by and large there was an unfettered freedom to do so – no one was in a position to challenge the 'experts'.

The costs of changing the information systems of companies to get them into a form which could be processed in terms of reorganization, stationery etc, new employment and retraining were colossal. The computer installations themselves were beset by teething troubles and as one followed the other so the manager complained that more staff were needed to iron them out. These were the days when every bus, tube station, or train carried pi diagram puzzles which asked the solver to contact the advertiser provided if he or she wanted a job in computers.

The vicious circle of spiralling costs, inadequate performance, very low-capacity utilization and a growing gap between the manufacturers' claims and the real results had to come to a halt. It did, in the late 1960s. Board members were given responsibility, staffing levels were reduced, and proper costing and work targets were set for D.P. departments. This cut-back, precipitated by a cash flow crisis throughout industry and commerce, saw the demise of many consultancies, computer

37

bureaux and 'time-sharing' operations. It also re-established some order amidst chaos and rehabilitated the reputation of the industry.

Far from there being an overall loss of jobs in the early years there was a marginal increase. Jobs in information systems and in the installation itself between them outnumbered the number of jobs replaced by the output of the computer. It must be remembered that computers were being very under-utilized as far as their capacity and their potential were concerned. Most companies or local and central government departments used them for the simple repetitive tasks of wages preparation, and invoicing – and precious little else. In some instances, however, the computer generated jobs though indirectly. In academic and research spheres the new tool widened the scope; calculations could be performed more quickly and the number of researchers and research lines increased with the number of installations.

The original computers also stimulated centralization of control and facilitated the trend to 'bigness' – a very popular concept in the 1960s. The ability to centralize and to standardize accounting systems, returns, sales, etc, from different companies, departments or whatever, opened up the possibility of mergers. Industrial concentration grew and with it redundancies, especially amongst middle and senior managements; government departments increased in size although the potential redundancies were offset by the increases in their responsibilities and thus their staffing. The net position was, even with these losses, positive in terms of jobs.

Today, however, the position is somewhat different. The systems of information gathering are well established and need little new manpower. In fact, as new software systems and techniques have come into wide operation so the need to maintain the existing level of staffing has diminished. The minicomputer (as opposed to the micro-computer) is being used by smaller and smaller enterprises and the new video display units and the 'real-time' mechanisms are starting to erode employment. Although much of this is organized through natural wastage and, in the main, is tending to involve clerical and administrative staff, salesmen, warehousemen, managers and some production staff are now losing their jobs.

The application of the computer principle also affected manual, especially craft, workers. The development of the numerically controlled machine (N.C.M.) and other tools such as the automatic welding machine led to redundancies amongst skilled engineers. Their adoption has been slow overall in Britain when compared with Japan or Germany, but they have been slowly making ground.

Work changes rather than a loss of jobs were the major effect of the introduction of the computer. New technologies inevitably mean that new skills are required and those employees with existing skills either have to retrain or become sidetracked on promotion ladders. Most people who were 40 years and upwards felt inadequate in the face of the new jargon and systems, and even if they volunteered or were selected for retraining, only managed to reach the lower levels of competence. Expectations of good careers were shattered and early voluntary retirements became a feature of the personnel scene. The same scenario was played out after take-overs occurred stimulated by the computer, especially in local authorities where the reorganization often meant that there were, for example, four borough or county surveyors for one post.

In the manual worker areas there were two repercussions. Skilled men, especially engineers, found themselves operating machines and acting in a semi-skilled or even unskilled capacity; salaries remained in the same brackets as did the job titles, but the jobs themselves became eminently less satisfying. Through their shop stewards manual workers' unions have traditionally attempted to control their working environment by controlling the speed at which production lines move or at which other processes have to be undertaken. The computer changed some in-work techniques and enabled, for example, the planning of component movements within a production cycle. This meant that the stewards lost an element of control partly because they were pre-empted and partly because of an inability or unwillingness to negotiate on the technical points that emerged.

The resulting changes affected the labour force quite profoundly. In the finance industries there was a dramatic increase in unionization as a protective measure against future uncertainties. Among skilled workers differentials started to become eroded partly because of a loss of bargaining power. Overall the ability of workers to predict and then control their working environment diminished and the need for measures for industrial democracy became clearer.

Contrary to first estimates, the introduction of the computer, along with all the changes that it stimulated, has exerted a considerable effect on work. This effect is still continuing and will do so in a cumulative manner. Yet it remains unfortunate that the computer attracted so much hysteria and foreboding. The United States were sufficiently concerned to set up a commission in 1966 which, amongst other things, looked at the impact of technology and automation on employment. This alone, although its actual findings were anodyne, was enough to stimulate some worrying thoughts. Because the actual effects of computerization and automation were not as dramatic as had been suggested a blasé effect has been created. It didn't happen before – it won't happen again. Unfortunately, despite the prevalence of this attitude, it is incorrect. The special circumstances surrounding the advent of the computer are unlikely to be repeated in the newer technological breakthroughs, especially in micro-electronics. These are more flexible, cheaper and need less labour to either produce, use or maintain. Above all many of the labour intensive systems that may be required have already been established to feed the computer. It is unlikely that those in charge of large or small organizations will repeat the same mistakes over control and manning – they have moved up and along the learning curve. Despite the fact that similarities between the computer and the microprocessor concerning work are fewer than the differences and the fact that all the above arguments are well known the myths continue even in high places. In a December 1978 document the government 'think tank' actually used the argument that as the computer did not cause unemployment nor would the micro-electronic revolution.

The big main frame computer and its development was, up to the advent of the microprocessor, the last of the major technical changes affecting work and consumers alike. It did not produce the structural unemployment that was feared, not only because of the reasons previously discussed, but also because it had significant technical limitations. Because of its size, the big main frame computer could only exercise its central controlling or its other functions at a distance from the site of operations; this lack of mobility limited its growth. Now the mini-computer has arrived but rather like the canal system, at precisely the wrong time. For the world is about to leap from the big main frame to the micro-chip based mini-computer, leaving the conventional mini a residual place in the history of technological change. Yet even in its short existence the smaller computer, along with newer and more reliable pre-programmed techniques, has led to some structural unemployment.

The introduction of the computer and Keynesian economics are not the only factors which give rise to prevailing wisdoms which suggest that there will not be a major problem. We believe that these, too, are wrong. Whether they refer to existing unemployment levels or to the nature of the employer–worker relationship, we believe that the disemployment consequences will move ahead inexorably.

At the time of writing this book there are roughly 1·5 million people registered as unemployed in Britain; there are 5·7 million unemployed in the E.E.C. and 17 million in the industrialized O.E.C.D. countries. Whilst much of this is the result of a deficiency of demand, there is a growing suspicion that a considerable minority is more fundamental, that is to say, even with expanded demand there will still overall be fewer jobs available. Add this on to the problem of diminishing profits for each new capital intensive investment and the basis of Keynesian economics as a long-term strategy is seriously weakened in a free enterprise system. Added to this is that any chance of increasing productivity is through the adoption of labour saving technology and that, on present evidence, this would not increase the return to capital.

Conventional economic policies have signally failed to prevent unemployment rising on a world-wide scale and in particular have failed to halt Britain's overall economic decline. We are also about to enter an era of profound technological change. If we look back over the last decade men have been to the moon, space probes have invaded Venus, weaponry has become more sophisticated and we now have 'test-tube babies', yet the work process has changed but slowly. The new technologies are those which can, and will, act as (this long overdue) catalysts for change.

The world changes and, despite the old French adage, never does remain the same. It has been argued that the objective conditions of work have not changed; that there are those who work and those who employ; a patently true statement. However this can go somewhat further, but in slightly different directions. The exploitation argument is a familiar and time hallowed one and in more extreme cases gets itself converted into the wage-slave syndrome. Surprisingly enough it was Kipling, not generally recognized as one of the world's most radical men, who first used the phrase. However radically one seeks to push this argument, and there are some whose logic takes them into the wilder shores of eclecticism, it contains an undeniable and fundamental truth and this remains the same whatever the technological change or work environment.

It cannot be denied that working in an air-conditioned, well-lit office is not the same as working down an eighteenth century pit, and work in a modern car plant is different from a nineteenth-century steelworks in physical characteristics, and dangers involved. There is still, however, the fact that it is work and basically whoever owns the enterprise, be it the state, a pension fund, an individual or a mega-corporation, people are doing this work for other people. The advent of the computer did not change this relationship and it is most unlikely that technical advances of any description will have such a fundamental effect. Technology has instead made many working lives considerably easier, extended life expectancy and enabled the ordinary person to live in a degree of comfort unbelievable to those who worked but 50 years ago. Whilst this may not satisfy political purists, it represents a very long leg of the forward march. Each step along the way has changed the working environment if not the attitude to work, and these changes are irreversible.

Responses to technology have been part and parcel of these changes. Technological innovation has been brought in by employers, not by workers. In every instance the unions representing the workers have had to adapt their thinking in order to prevent work changes to the detriment of their members, or redundancies. It must be said that in some instances this defence has been neither tough enough nor adequately informed.

The new technological changes will, as we shall see, have to elicit a powerful intellectual response from the trade union movement and a moment's thought will be sufficient to recognize the difference between short- and long-term responses. Well organized trade unions in any country hold the keys to the quality of life in that country and thus have a great responsibility. If the world is about to change, certainly as regards the balance of work and leisure there will not only have to be changes in the trade union movements, but in the political institutions too. The adaptation will almost certainly be painful in all senses. We have already seen industrial disputes in West Germany preceding the introduction of radical new work systems and this will undoubtedly be an inevitable response. Overall, the changes in method will challenge existing knowledge and the existing power-vested interests in all branches of society, and this, in itself, is a destabilizing process.

Over the past two centuries this process has been going on. In the last 20 years its pace has increased, but over the next 20 years the speed of change will make that of the previous 200 years appear like the Wright brothers' machine when compared with Concorde. Societies have adapted because the time they had to react was lengthy, or the changes were not that fundamental and the period of great change brought forth the great movements – the Chartists and the Labour Party in Britain. One thing is certain, there will be further change – what is uncertain is how we will cope with it nationally and internationally in the time we have at our disposal.

4 The third Industrial Revolution?

Revolution is a word with disturbing connotations. It antici-pates the upsetting of traditional systems, values and relation-ships. As such it is the subject of much apprehension for most and a cause of excitement and anticipation for a few.

The first industrial revolution was stimulated by a radical development in the power system to drive machinery. The second was based on a combination of a further change in power and a breakthrough in transportation. The third, which has just started, will be based on information and communications but, as with the previous two, the technologies involved are capable of wider applications and a deeper penetration into the fabric of society.

Although mankind has developed more sophisticated methods of prediction than perusing an animal's entrails, we can only make educated guesses as to what the future might bring in economics, in politics and in business. No one can say with absolute certainty that the silicon chip based information revolution will ever reach its full potential or indeed what that potential might be. Nevertheless the probability is that micro-processor technology will ultimately swamp all before it.

Microprocessor technology masquerades under a series of different names and definitions. Silicon chip technology is the most well known but 'very large scale integration' or V.L.S.I. is another; a branch of 'semiconductor technology', 'information technology' and 'disseminated data processing' take their place in the list. But whatever the name the technology remains the same.

This whole technology is relatively new, although it is merely an extension of the use and theory of transistors. This was in itself a vital technical breakthrough which changed the pattern of production on a world-wide scale in the radio and television industries as well as making possible the growth of computers. The semiconductor industry, which is really just the exploitation of the property of materials like silicon of only partly conducting electricity, based on the transistor alone, developed as early as 1952/3. Integrated circuits, that is, the combination of various parts, transistors themselves, resistors, diodes etc, all in one silicon chip is as recent as 1963. Although the technology has been known for some time, industrially it has only been in existence for 16 years and only really taken off in the last 5 years, although integrated circuits have been used for longer.

Technological breakthroughs cannot be predicted any more accurately than can the future. It is tempting to ascribe the success of research to the amount of money made available but there is no necessary correlation. However, it must be true that the more money there is available, the more experiments there will be conducted by a larger number of better qualified people. Fundamental research is very different to applied research or development studies. The microprocessor and its applications are a case in point.

Basic new ideas are often generated at universities or publicly financed research institutions rather than in either corporations or government departments. What companies or governments, especially in the armaments industry, are good at is applied research and development. Generally an end product is held firmly in mind and it is in this area of research that the vast expenditures tend to take place.

Micro-electronics took off as a serious study because the United States Agency (N.A.S.A.) and the Department of Defence needed foolproof, miniaturized computer systems. Conventional computers were too large and heavy to be adapted as the guidance systems of space capsules and rockets. Vast sums of money were pumped into U.S. industries to solve this problem. This emerged as the printing of micro-circuits on to tiny chips of silicon. Since then the technology has developed rapidly and it seems perfectly plausible that 1 million transistors and other components on one silicon chip measuring 1 square centimetre could be manufactured in the 1980s – up to 250,000 are being designed now. Through the appropriate agencies the

United States Government has poured over 1 billion dollars into this research, development and manufacture.

'Chips' are not the only form of micro-electronics. The magnetic bubble memory is another, though at present its environment needs more careful regulation than standard uses will allow, and acoustic waves and grooves are also available. It is not inconceivable that by the time this book is published at least half a dozen more carriers will have been announced, though not all might be viable in the market place.

The cost of manufacturing silicon chips is both high and low. If this sounds contradictory it is because of the peculiar nature of the process. Each micro-circuit has to be printed on to the silicon, correctly aligned, assembled and tested. Thus the capital costs needed to set up a 'chip' plant are very high. Very sophisticated machinery is needed and the greater the number of components on a chip the more sophisticated (and expensive) the machinery has to become. Designs may become more complex, miniaturization more minute and power per square centimetre may increase but machinery and techniques have to be developed so as to match each new advance. Lasers of special forms are now being employed in the manufacture – each of which is the result of substantial research and development expenditure in its own right. The initial capital costs are thus huge. However, the marginal costs – or variable costs – are extraordinarily low and this results in what accountants call front-loading; the expenditure is almost all at the beginning. The cost of chips has fallen dramatically but seems now stabilized at less than 5 U.S. dollars each. The nature of the costs inevitably means that the greater the production runs, the lower the cost per chip.

The basic research and the initial manufacturing of the 'chip' started in the so-called 'Silicon Valley' outside San Jose in California. Each of the pioneering companies was small and the subsequent hiving off into new companies, from these, which together have trebled the number of enterprises and removed some from California, has meant that they individually are still small. This is not surprising since it was a new concept and a new challenge, which demanded more flexibility and imagination, not only from the technologists and scientists but also from the management staffs.

Large corporations, on the other hand, whether public or private, build up their own innate conservatism, often exemplified by the internal traditions they observe. This fosters an environment where enterprise can rock the boat, disturb promotion patterns, and go unappreciated by a board which has to think of the shareholders and its own future. A new unproven technology with high initial costs will have little attraction for a large, successful company. Its capital can be put to less risky projects yielding a steady return. Only after all the spadework has been done will this type of company 'move in' and attempt to take over or merge with the pioneer.

Chip manufacture is as important as the production of a basic raw material like coal or oil. For which reason the National Enterprise Board should be applauded for deciding to facilitate their manufacture within the United Kingdom. It is not merely a matter of strategic or defence importance, although both factors are important. Indeed, if anything confirms the view that this technology is here to stay, it is the public argument that Britain cannot be at the mercy of foreign suppliers. But the mass production of chips has two important side-effects. The first is that a body of highly skilled men and women will be built up on the small existing base and this hopefully will enable teaching and planning to go ahead in the U.K. The second is that by producing the raw material we will encourage its use and subsequent research and developments. In the same way that it is rare for a non-volume car manufacturing country to have a large car component industry, so the commercial exploitation of micro-electronics should become that much more likely. Even if the U.K. chip manufacturing concern makes losses over the first decade of its life the initiative is likely to have overall beneficial economic effects.

At present supply of silicon chip manufacture exceeds demand. Even so it is unlikely that the price per chip will fall much further over the next few years. What *will* fall is the cost per function. This is because it is a rule of thumb in the industry that the capacity of an integrated circuit will quadruple every 2 years (and it has) and thereby increase the number of transistors and other components. In turn this means that fewer integrated circuits are required and less packaging and other software for most outside manufacturers, that is, those companies to whom the chips are sold, all these items are great cost-savers. Mass production is vital.

What has so far been suggested about microprocessor technology is based on the assumption that on average there now appears to be a 15 year gap between discovery and commercial acceptance and viability of a new technology, the larger part of this period being required for development purposes. This was certainly true of the transistor itself. It therefore follows that the new breakthrough is upon us now as the interregnum period has well and truly expired. It is also probable that this new technology will itself stimulate the shortening of this period for new developments.

The basic mass-produced chip will be produced in a highly competitive industry, as regards both price and technical efficiency. The industry will also be working in a climate of remarkably rapid change. Thus, after, say, the first 10 years, there will be a wholesale rationalization of the industry with the creation of larger units or an absorption of producers by larger customers. Clearly too the mass market demand will be for standard products, perhaps up to ten different types, and this will encourage mergers. However, there will be a market demand for the larger and more complex custom-built integrated circuitry. In other words the chip will be available in an upmarket version and the more common supermarketable type.

Obviously the more complex upmarket version is likely to satisfy an overall smaller demand than the standard; the standard, however, could be marketed not only on a price basis but on a size and reliability basis. But both types are becoming increasingly important by comparison with the very low costs as against those of conventional electronic circuitry.

Industrial revolutions are not created merely by the invention of a new product, however ingenious it might be. That product must be capable of use and in a myriad of ways. Its price must also make its adoption feasible within current price constraints, or preferably actually cut prices or increase profits. On both counts integrated circuits are winners.

They can be used in four basic ways. They can serve as the basis for new products, for example, watches, calculators and word processors; they can replace conventional circuitry in existing products such as car components; they can change the productive process itself, for example, robotics; and they can affect basic information systems, for example, system X in telecommunications. When looking at this prospect commentators tend to restrict their comments to one, or at the most two, of these uses and often in a way that either reinforces the prejudices of the reader or shocks him out of apathy. Robots in car plants are often described to the exclusion of all else, whether in union or engineering journals or on information uses in the appropriate technical press. It is a crippling limitation that so few people, other than academics, look at the technology in the round. For it is this very capacity to act on the whole, rather than on one isolated sector, that gives this particular technology its revolutionary potential.

Just as information and comments are fragmented, so is a parallel division between economic and technical analysis. Economists continue to analyse their data, especially when looking at economy-wide statistics in the medium term as though all past investment has been neutral and will remain so. The possibility that £1 million of new investment could have a totally different job impact this year, as compared to last year, is only tenable if there is a quantum leap in technology, and economic models do not take this into account. The technical press on the other hand tends to ignore or under-evaluate the wider economic and social implications of the introduction of micro-circuitry and concentrate almost exclusively on the individual process in question. Both attitudes tend to make a wide-ranging analysis of the situation that much more difficult for non-experts. While some attempts have been made to combine the full range of issues, notably in a B.B.C. TV Horizon series programme 'Now the Chips are Down', the major arguments have gone by default because of the peculiarly British syndrome of compartmentalization.

The most visible signs of this new technology are, quite appropriately, those that the public at large can recognize. At present there are two major and two minor uses. The digital watch has swept all before it. Within the last 5 years it has completely changed an industry that had remained virtually unaltered since the invention of the balance wheel. From being a gimmick and a high cost one at that, the digital watch has now become the standard lower cost conventional watch. To the consumer it is cheaper, more reliable, more durable and, given consumer fickleness, more fashionable. The scale of impact has administered a severe shock to an international industry which had complacently watched its profits automatically mount. The public often associates this novel form of watch with a digital display (the fashionable aspect), but this type of drive also features in conventional watches with ordinary hands. In less than 10 years 49 per cent of the world production of watches has switched over to electronics and quartz and the technical development is by no means at an end.

The conventional watch industry was totally unprepared for the challenge and in great measure it succumbed. The Lip factory workers' work-in and co-operative in France foundered on the rocks of the new technology, not on its day-to-day managerial expertise. The Swiss watch industry, vital to the national balance of payments as well as a major employer, lost at least 25 per cent of its labour force and saw a 'turnaround' in its balance of payments to the extent of £125 million per year.

But it is worth looking at the effects of this industry-wide change in more detail since they may well indicate something of the future developments and the problems associated with the new technology. The traditional watch manufacturers and their wholesale and retail outlets did not believe that such an invasion into their markets was possible and, even if it was, did not see how it could succeed. From comments made by British manufacturers in areas already threatened by foreign competition using micro-electronics, this complacency appears to be relatively widespread over a substantial range of industries. Such an attitude, however, does leave a manufacturer totally unprepared for what is essentially a predictable eventuality. Old and trusted techniques, however quaint and historically desirable, are not proof against foreign, technologically based competition. The second and associated result of the digital watch revolution was heavy price and non-price competition. As prices fell so the functions associated with a watch increased. Stop-watch facilities, date, day, year, alarm systems and memory systems were all offered for the same price as conventional watches.

Almost overnight the international structure of the watch industry was changed, with inevitable repercussions on the balance of trade in several countries. At the same time the traditional watch making countries found themselves short of skilled manpower in both design and production phases and this delayed any possible real response, while new producer countries such as South Korea and Japan, not bound by tradition, have found it easy to recruit or train the necessary labour. Finally, though the total market increased, turnover decreased and labour had to be shed at all levels. Of course the watch revolution could be described as an extreme example and it could be claimed that there exist few, if any, similar products which could be so dramatically affected. But the desk calculator disproves that. Once a flourishing highly labour intensive, high cost product, this has been totally killed by the micro-electronic based pocket calculator. In all respects calculators have followed watches. Unawareness, intense price competition, even more intense non-price product quality competition and easy use, have altered fundamentally international production and made many skills redundant. The giant United States National Cash Register company got into financial difficulties because it did not recognize the trend early enough.

The second major way in which the public recognize micro-electronics is in the digital display. Whether this is on watch or clock faces, on taxi meters, on car dashboards or on petrol pumps, it is obvious that something has changed. The technological breakthrough underpinning it may not be recognized, but an awareness of change is present. In a minor sense the public has, again unknowingly, realized the changes possible with the advent of TV games and of the teletext type systems such as Ceefax and Oracle, neither have yet exerted a major impact, yet they differ sufficiently from past practice to be the subject of much comment. All of these four, however, share one thing in common, and that is that they are all new products and all highly visible. This will not necessarily be the case with the majority of uses to which the microprocessor can be put.

We have already subdivided the uses of microprocessors into those going into *products* and those into (or controlling) processes. We also distinguished between microprocessors

51

stimulating a *new product* and those which amend an existing product. They have one other potential function. They may create a new market by replacing an existing product. For example, the new generation of computers is a new version of an old product – replacing it *and* looking to a new market. This set of distinctions, unsophisticated though it might be, is essential to produce an adequate analysis of the effects of the technology on work and employment.

Where, in fact, is the chip being used? Beginning with products found in and around a home, almost anything with a conventional electrical motor and control system is using or will use silicon chips. Washing machines and dish-washers, electric cookers (indeed gas cookers), sewing machines, electric irons, central heating systems, TV sets, TV games, mixers and mincers, hi-fi equipment, cassette recorders and clocks are *all* having microprocessors incorporated. Microprocessors control, make cycles work smoothly and provide the automatic pre-setting elements. They cannot be seen, yet have simplified the productive process, enabled slimmer or less bulky design, provided durability and reliability and thus cut down servicing costs. The incorporation of the micro-chip based integrated circuit into these goods is by no means complete; indeed, those produced in Britain have a very low content at present.

In cars alone micro-electronics will undertake several functions. It is confidently predicted that in 1979–80 the major United States manufacturers will be offering mass-produced cars at similar real prices to today, but incorporating three or four of the following systems as standard: digital dashboard display, braking and servo systems, ignition control, clutch control, exhaust emission control, carburettor, fuel injection or petrol pump control and, perhaps slightly later than sooner, diagnostic and collision sensor systems. If the U.S. is provided with these for its home market the European subsidiaries will not be far behind and then the indigenous producers, Renault, Fiat, Volkswagen and British Leyland will also have to follow, or go under. As with household equipment, their introduction will go largely unnoticed; they are not new products. Other equipment such as cameras, projectors, greenhouse control and video-tape machines, let alone electric toothbrushes and carving knives are all capable of extensive improvement.

The actual mechanics of production can be divided into two; those affecting industrial situations and those affecting the office – clerical, administrative and managerial functions. In addition there is the semi-industrial sector employed in testing and measuring equipment. Taking the office first, there are word processors – and in the near future there will be fully electronic typewriters, accounting machines, intelligent terminals, desk top micro-computers, high-speed copiers and facsimile provisions, telephone answering systems and dictating systems, mail sorting and collation machines. All are already in use in various parts of the world including the U.K.

The ability to act as a control mechanism in the industrial sector provides an even larger prospective list. Much of it is devoted to the scaling and then the control of sequences in the productive process, so that some of its functions are as much supervisory and managerial as manual. The current uses are for batch control of fluids or bulk solids, machine tool control, materials handling, storage and warehousing systems, welding machine control, electroplating, painting and spraying control, health and safety emission monitoring and robotics or automation replacing all sorts of equipment in the textiles, printing, cars, TV and manufacturing industries.

It is this ability to be programmed for control functions that makes the silicon chip such a potent force as both a cheap component and in the production process itself. On the testing and equipment side they are now being incorporated in scanners, X-ray equipment, biochemical analysis machines, oscilloscopes for all uses, and environmental supervisors and for analyses of all descriptions.

The health services are starting to rely heavily on this more sophisticated equipment, but costs will have to fall, or National Health Service budgets rise, before the United Kingdom takes a real leap forward. Defence industries, from radar to missile control and from war games to navigation and telecommunications, are probably the U.K.'s largest user of the new microcircuitry and certainly the largest user in the U.S.A. and, by extrapolation, in the Soviet Union too. The field of education, from teaching aids for those learning to read, to those doing post-doctoral research, is another slowly growing, but potentially huge market.

The semi-public debate as to whether or when System X, an electronic switching system, should be introduced into the British exchanges has alerted many to the possibility of a new and more efficient telephone system. It is, however, only a starting point in the possibilities that very large-scale integration opens up in the whole field of communications. It is a viable system and it works well wherever it has been introduced. Other known and used telecommunication devices include telex facilities, Viewdata and Ceefax transmission, teletypewriters and time division packet transmission.

Telecommunications and computers of all descriptions go hand-in-hand because one enhances the abilities of the other. This partnership, along with the uses to which it can be put, herald the 'information society'. Information is a vital resource; it is also non-depleting. When gathered or disseminated the sum total of information not only does not fall, like oil, gas or minerals, but generally increases, because of the feedback to the original information. Communication of information is vital to business, medicine, government, personal lives and especially in education. Most of this is handled currently on paper in the form of books, memoranda or newspapers. This is not only inefficient but also very costly in terms of the labour involved and the environmental damage of tree consumption.

It is now possible to envisage a system where textual or main source information, that is, the written word, is carried on almost entirely through a single system of electrical signals. As well as microprocessors, there can be involved optical fibres, and the large main frame computer stores of knowledge ('databases'). Information has to be processed, communicated and stored. The electronic typewriter is capable of transmitting its typed message either direct to an individual recipient, or to a computer terminal for storage. The message is automatically filed, brought forward, discarded, or wiped out. Drawing on these combined processes the telephone system could be changed out of all recognition. As about 80 per cent of calls are local – not trunk – the system is costly in terms of short distance and short duration calls. But it is possible to have a telephone system which will store messages until a critical number is reached and then automatically transmitted – this is known as 'packet switching': the technique is nothing more than an electronic postman! Although an international protocol has been signed on this technique, the costs are still high and will remain so until such time as locally based systems come into operation dispensing with the large existing computer-controlled systems.

One method of doing this which would enable both households and offices to participate more fully in an information society is to 'convert' the buildings concerned for information into a main terminal and sub-terminals along the lines of normal electric services. If this sounds dramatic, expensive and therefore a non-starter, one should bear in mind that North Sea gas conversion was completed over the whole country on a house-to-house basis, on schedule and with the minimum of fuss and bother; similarly houses and blocks of flats have easily been wired for cable or piped television. If tackled on a similar area-to-area basis, there is no reason why information ring main systems should not be a standard feature of new dwellings, offices and plants, and also of conversions in the case of existing ones. Again the technologies themselves are known and proven.

In considering the impact of micro-electronics on the computer and data-processing industry, it is important to realize that it is acting upon what is already a growth area. Yet, apart from the point-of-sale terminals in supermarkets and the visual display units in airline offices, this is an operation almost totally hidden from the public. Most of the advances are highly complex and technical in nature, but some, like intelligent terminals, micro-computers and mini-computers are already being used and, more to the point, have started to exist in the public consciousness, while others like 'front-end' processors and magnetic disc control have stimulated a public awareness. However much the public knows, or is interested in, is not immediately relevant. What is, is that the changes *are* being made and the new systems *are* becoming standard.

The micro-computer has not yet emerged. In theory one chip could act as a fully fledged computer of some considerable power, and indeed that development cannot be far away as it is really a matter of having the softwear industry catch up. So far most of the chip's uses discussed have been based on a 'custom-built' version, with its set of instructions and functions already defined. But the micro-computer is the programmable chip and its charm is that it is so much more flexible than the specific type. Although it is not difficult for the technical experts to envisage a combination of these two properties in one chip, it is more likely that microprocessors will be used in mini-computers rather than act as free standing computers in their own right.

One property of this new technology requires expansion. It is dynamic: which makes it even more difficult to predict its future consequences. For when used on computer systems themselves the chip becomes a new technology which enables us to solve problems and produce other technologies; the chip *acts as a technological catalyst*. It even enables us to contemplate the possibility of new technologies. However, unless time scales dramatically shorten it seems likely that few brand new technologies will be productively in use before 1990.

Integrated circuits, semiconductors, silicon chips, microprocessors are all going to have the most enormous impact as has been described, albeit sketchily, and the brunt of this will initially be felt by the work process – or lack of it. All sectors of society are affected – some fundamentally more than others. But it is not the only new technology which will have an impact, even if, in its ubiquity, it will far outweigh the others.

Of these, probably nuclear power, genetic engineering and microbiology are the most interesting and most far-reaching. Nuclear power has been used in a practical and constructive form for at least 15 years. Its energy is used to propel ships and submarines, and to generate electricity. But its very reputation as a hideously destructive force, and its longer-term radiation hazards must affect societies' view of it. (Britain is amazingly tolerant in this respect.) This international reaction may restrict (certainly in the short and medium terms) nuclear energy from fulfilling its full potential. This attitude clashes strongly with the Common Market Commission proposals for a large build-up of such sources of energy production. Within this reaction there is an important insight: people may trade-off technical progress and a better standard of living for certainty and safety.

Genetic engineering is hardly less threatening, although it is associated by the public with disaster. It therefore has only recently become public knowledge, partly due to concerns voiced after the 1978 Birmingham University smallpox disaster, and although some countries have set up monitoring systems, it has a frighteningly destructive potential. The principle is to transplant the chromosomes or character-forming parts of one cell into another to create a totally new entity. For example, an oil debris-eating bacillus is envisaged which would obviate the cleaning and the replacement of oilfield piping and equipment. Work is also going on at present to 'adapt' the common bacterium of the gut so that it produces insulin to aid diabetic sufferers. The major companies, such as I.C.I., are sufficiently convinced of the practicality of these and other projects to set up special development units and to devote major resources to research in genetic engineering.

There are plants in the world that fix nitrogen from the air through their leaves into the soil. Suppose these could be made to cross-fertilize, either in a micro-biological way, or by genetic engineering with cereal and rice crops to provide for self-fertilization of the soil? The sales of nitrogenous fertilizers could be slashed. This is no pipe-dream. It is actively being worked upon now.

This chapter has mapped out the probability of the third industrial revolution. It has not looked at the changes in depth, nor has it examined the work implications, for both issues will be explored in later chapters. But the present evidence surely demonstrates that the case for anticipating the coming radical change is overwhelming; that the technological explosion has happened; and that what is needed now is a guarantee that the fall-out will be beneficial. Was this the case in the first industrial revolution? Misery was the consequence of that, although in the long term it formed the basis of present-day living standards. This poses a problem in differences between short- and long-term responses in social and especially economic terms. But, before analysing the effects of the information revolution, it is necessary to set it in its context of the United Kingdom economy, to avoid considering change in isolation from its environment.

5 *The economic background*

We live in nation states, each with its own history, customs and attitudes. Each state sets out to run its economy to satisfy its own requirements, striving for those objectives to which national political parties give priority. But all these individual states are exposed in some way or another to external forces and influences, both political and economic. There are no closed economies and trade, although not conducted primarily on a world-wide basis by many countries, is strongly multilateral; even those countries within trading blocs – the E.E.C. or Comecon, for example – now trade extensively outside of their defined boundaries. Consequently when world trade is sluggish, the management of individual economies is made more difficult and national objectives or aspirations are often delayed or frustrated.

For world trade to continue smoothly the large balances or deficits in individual countries will have to be 'smoothed out'. It is when all countries' economies are just in balance that the world economy will attain its ideal structure. Every country's export is another's import – unless it happens to be the E.E.C.'s 'butter carousel' – and no state can keep running up deficits year after year even with devaluation as an economic tool. If the latter state of affairs develops then the deficit country will ultimately have to restrict its imports by either slowing down its own economy or putting up barriers to entry. In turn this means that the exporting country will suffer from reduced exports and world trade will begin to slow in the short term.

The world today has two major industrial countries with embarrassingly large trade surpluses, Japan and West Germany. It also has one major country, the U.S.A., with an equally embarrassingly large trade deficit and the United States is crucial to any world economic policy. It is at present and, for the conceivable future, will remain, the major manufacturing nation both in terms of imports and exports, and also is the major agricultural surplus producer. Without a recovery in the United States' balance of payments the prospects for reasonable world economic growth are limited even if, which is unlikely, Germany and Japan correct their positive imbalances.

For the United Kingdom the growth in world trade is more vital than for most other developed countries, a fact which stems from the peculiar nature of the economy and its unique problems.

Like any other dynamic process the economy can conveniently be subdivided into time spans: short, medium and long term. Precise definitions are inappropriate inasmuch as forecasts over the period are themselves imprecise, but in general the short term is seen as covering periods of up to 2 years, the medium periods up to 5 years, and the long term up to Armageddon. Such distinctions are important for analysis, but tend to produce structural rigidities and to spur false arguments.

Since by definition any long-term analysis must range over a time-span which includes both short and medium terms, in a 20 year period there will fall ten short-term periods and five medium periods. Thus no policy predictions can be made over a long period without taking into account the possible short-term responses within that period. Unfortunately all that techniques of economic analysis can currently undertake is to lay down a strategy over the long term and then point out that tactics in the short and medium terms should interplay with, rather than oppose, those long-term ambitions.

British economic policy has continuously been a series of short-term reactions, primarily aimed at enabling the balance of payments actually to balance. If any longer-term strategy existed, and only once, in George Brown's plan in the 1964–6 Labour Government, has anything of the kind been publicly spelt out in detail, it would have been swamped by the short-term contingency steps as was George Brown's plan and his Ministry of Economic Affairs. This is almost certainly an inevitable consequence of the system binding the government and its relationships, or lack of them, with all the varied economic groups within the nation.

This preoccupation with the balance of payments is the reason this chapter opened with a discussion of world trade. At present it is sluggish, even slow, and is giving enough cause for concern to have stimulated two world economic summits and innumerable meetings between finance ministers and the International Monetary Fund.

Conventional wisdom suggests that the problem arose in 1973 when the Opec cartel suddenly raised the price of oil by a multiple of five in two stages. The effect on internal costs and inflation in many countries and on the balance of payments was clearly radical. Collectively the Opec countries ran up huge surpluses overnight and despite attempts to recycle them by widescale purchasing in the industrialized countries and promises of aid to the less-developed countries (L.D.C.s) these, by and large, still exist. To the same extent, however, the imbalance problem has resolved itself in that the price of oil since this period has not kept pace with inflation in the rest of the world. But the adverse balances and the rates of inflation took most countries by surprise and as a result most retrenched, cut government spending, increased taxes, reduced money supply and instituted incomes policies, all programmes designed to cut aggregate demand. Both the World Bank and the International Monetary Fund proselytized this method and did so up to 1977 when they suddenly realized that there were gravely undesirable side-effects. Primarily, of course, unemployment was growing world-wide. Most unusually then the World Bank actually asked governments to adopt mildly expansionist policies – an almost unheard of piece of banking advice.

Yet in fact, it is quite clear that this is not the whole story. Growth rates in nearly all western industrialized countries were falling well before the oil price crisis, even in or perhaps especially in, Western Germany. Britain was certainly no exception to this phenomenon. We argued earlier that the immediate postwar years up to the middle 1960s were the aberrant period with new products combining with reconstruction to provide an enormous economic boost. The slowdown from the mid-1960s onwards would tend to reinforce this interpretation.

Increasingly, investment has been undertaken neither to

produce new products nor launch new materials but to increase the efficiency of the existing system of production. This in turn has meant that investment was resulting in the mounting of more capital-intensive operations and depressing the demand for labour. Competition between companies is now in terms of reliability and style as much as price and delivery, important though all are. Clearly some countries, notably West Germany with its relatively high priced goods, trade successfully by drawing on other comparative advantages. In other words, capital deepening rather than capital widening has recently been taking place. Some corroboration of this view is to be found in the 1977 McCracken Report conducted on behalf of the O.E.C.D. which looks, among other things, into invest-ment and technology. In all of the major industrial countries the percentage of investment for new industrial buildings in indus-trial investment as a whole has declined dramatically. The investment that has been taking place has been to provide new equipment, using new efficient techniques rather than spread-ing into new plant to produce for larger markets. The exception is the U.K., but here new industrial building has been at a significantly lower level than in other countries for some twenty years. Another interesting piece of evidence is from West Ger-many, where surveys are regularly conducted on the type of investment undertaken. In 1960 54 per cent of industrial investment was for the expansion of capacity; by 1970 this had fallen to 40 per cent and in 1977 it had collapsed to 15 per cent. This means that in 1977, 85 per cent of West German invest-ment was to improve existing plant and machinery and, given the new technologies available, this has been at the expense of jobs. Internationally there is also a lack of demand for those traditional goods and services on which most industrialized economies are based, and until such time as this is thought to be about to improve no investment will be made to expand capac-ity. But even this argument is flawed. The new equipment *now* installed is not, in general terms, being used in anything like an optimal fashion; there is a great deal of spare capacity. This of course varies from industry to industry, company by company and as between countries, but it does mean that production can be easily expanded *without* the employment of more people.

The problem is both world-wide and structural, and stems

from, paradoxically, a lack of fundamental innovation and technical change in the post-war industries on which the post-war boom was based. This absence of change has been in terms of the product rather than on the component or manufacturing process side, both of which have altered and both of which will alter considerably given the micro-electronic revolution. Although companies have tried brand image-making, built-in obsolescence, style changes and market manipulation, the market is remarkably static at its peak and all the above efforts have led only to saturation. There is a limit to the number of cars families need, or the perceived advantages of octophonic as opposed to stereophonic sound. Granted, income distribution is such that a substantial number of people have not yet been able to purchase one car or stereo-system let alone more than one, or a replacement, but even this potential market would not give the growth needed to match that of the 1950–60 period. In any event the required change in income distribution is at present not on the horizon, and indeed if work does collapse, will, unless radical political decisions are taken, be put back even farther. The post-1945 economic growth was centred around seven sectors: consumer durables, electronic goods, capital goods, synthetic and organic chemicals, oil refining, gas and electricity and·pharmaceuticals. These sectors cover a multitude of industries and products and they should be examined in some detail as the argument of saturation/slow growth has usually only been applied to older industries such as shipbuilding, textiles or railways.

The consumer durable industries 'took-off' in the 1950s as real incomes rose and credit facilities developed. Of course attention must be directed not only at the primary industry, but also at the component and supplier industries. Production and assembly of these types of goods is internationalized through the transnational company and any slowing down is therefore felt simultaneously in several countries. This high gearing or domino effect makes it all the more difficult for any single country to take steps against the collapse of work. Among consumer durables will be found cars, refrigerators, washing machines, furniture, cleaners, and all those domestic electrical appliances up to electric blankets and toothbrushes. A high percentage of sales in this category is now replacement rather than new purchase and the growth rates during the last decade reflect the steady erosion of producer expectations. Electronic goods, the second category, partially overlap with consumer durables through such items as TV sets and hi-fi equipment, but they also include computers themselves, electronic instruments and test machinery, and communications equipment. As with consumer durables this category has experienced a degree of market saturation, but within it there lie both some growth areas and areas of high potential growth – though not necessarily concomitant with a growth of jobs.

Capital goods industries have great spare capacity worldwide because of the fact that they reflect the lack of overall investment. Yet the new technologies will revolutionize the entire industry and growth, already evident in Japan and West Germany, is expected to take place over the next decade. This, however, is not the case in the synthetic materials industries. These encompass a variety of products from synthetic cloths to plastics, P.V.C., synthetic rubbers and all the packaging and other products for which these are used. This has been one of the major growth industries since the war but is currently suffering with vast spare capacity and a substantial number of plant closures. Clearly the market remains but growth depends on new areas of substitution. Steel is a vulnerable material and it is highly probable that car manufacturers will use synthetic fibres for body shells, but even so overall the producers do not expect to return to the earlier growth rates.

The energy industries grew very rapidly in the early post-war period. Power stations, natural gas, nuclear energy and oil all displayed high investment and high capital formation. Whilst the current depression has obviously reduced this growth, it is also true that the rate had slackened prior to 1973. The initial industrial take-off requirements have been met as indicated by the restricted demand for replacements and the slow expected growth. The latter is reflected in the Central Electricity Generating Board's forward plans which provide for little new plant, and the Board's patent unwillingness to expedite the building of the Drax B power station. In turn, since the oil refining industry is itself dependent upon growth in the car and transport, plastics and chemical industries, and as these are growing more slowly, so too will oil extraction and refining. But

63

the future dominated by the world-wide glut of refinery capacity which exists today, is made even more difficult by the current concern over resource depletion and the consequent fuel saving measures and technologies now being introduced.

The growth in pharmaceuticals was stimulated by the advances in microbiology, to a great extent centred, then and now, around the production of synthetic antibiotics. But molecular roulette, as it is called, is now yielding diminishing returns and to maintain profits prices are kept artificially high. In addition, more stringent statutory testing procedures in both U.S.A. and the U.K. must slow down the rate of product innovation making it uneconomic to develop the marginally useful product. In turn this has repercussions on the oil refinery industries.

In all, we thus have the situation where the main expansion industries since the 1945 war are suffering simultaneously a decline in their growth rates. Yet it is *growth* that is needed, as the McCracken Report itself agrees, if unemployment is to be reduced. Even without technological change actually reducing the number of people needed, where is this growth going to come from?

In this contest anyway growth is clearly not a precise enough word. It is only too conceivable for the gross domestic product of a country to grow at an annual rate in excess of 5 per cent and still have, indeed reinforce, growing unemployment. For there to be meaningful discussions or analysis of the unemployment problem we will need a new economic measure of partial growth. Investment leading to job-creative growth should be distinguished from investment that is either neutral or job destructive; what we really need are new measures of growth say $G1$, $G2$ and $G3$ with respect to employment, in the same way as we have different measures of money supply.

As suggested in Chapter 3, the Keynesians would now claim that the markets themselves would respond or could be made to respond. Demand is infinite and all that is needed is either the fiscal policy or slightly more direct intervention to enable the spare capacity in the economy to be taken up again. However, if that investment (and in this instance technologically oriented investment to create new demands) is dependent on profit or profit expectations, neither, in present circumstances, appear to be sufficiently high. In fact profit has been declining in most industrial countries over the past 20 years (not just in Britain) and as most surveys reveal expectations are low. Even if investment was forthcoming, however, it is likely that the number of jobs created in whatever sector is chosen, including the service sector, would be less than there would have been prior to the micro-electronic revolution.

The above considerations apply to all industrialized countries; what about the special problems of Britain? First and foremost it is a weak economy. The growth rate has been exceptionally low over the past 20 years, both investment and productivity are low. Large sectors of manufacturing industry have declined to a state of almost total non-existence, and others are working, at best, marginally. The environment has not been conducive to investment: successive stop-go policies have choked off demand as the balance of payments moved into deficit and industrialists have found it easier to invest abroad rather than in the U.K. When the next boom started the ability of industry to respond was impaired accordingly and manufactured and semi-manufactured goods had to be imported. In turn this led to an even faster balance of payments deficit, then an even shorter boom – a contraction of demand – and low investment, and with the next upturn even more imports. Pressure on sterling added to this vicious circle and this pressure led first to devaluation and then to a downward float of the pound. All of which made imports more expensive, and added to inflation whilst the expected compensatory increase in exports rarely materialized, thus adding to both balance of payments and overall competitive difficulties.

Britain is an economy peculiarly dominated by transnational companies. The United Nations Index, which compares the volume of exports with the volume of goods produced by nationally owned companies overseas, places Britain second after the United States. Only Britain and the U.S.A. had a ratio of over one. This is not a measure of foreign owned transnational company operations, although Britain has more than its fair share of those; rather it is a measure of British companies who chose to invest and produce abroad rather than domestically. Some argue that such overseas investment diminishes the drive to export in that exports then have to compete with the same company's overseas production. Whilst by no means universally accepted, this would explain the fact that both the U.K. and the U.S. do not get the increase in exports which forecasters suggest would follow devaluation.

Britain thus has a weak and weakening industrial base and this makes it very vulnerable to imports. North Sea oil acts as a mask for this state of affairs. It is giving and will continue to give 'turnaround' on the balance of payments of around £3 billion per year. This means that it is possible to expand demand in the economy appreciably before running into deficit difficulties. Negatively it means that Britain will not be allowed to take unilateral trade action to protect ailing industries because the general reason for such a dispensation is a chronic balance of payments problem. North Sea oil revenues are a new factor. These arise from the petroleum revenue tax (P.R.T.), licence fees and British National Oil Corporation reserves and are estimated to be in the region of £3 or £4 billion per year. The precise figures cannot be determined until the price of oil, the relative energy prices and the depletion rates are all known. Into this situation will come the microprocessor and its adjuncts, and it is very possible that this new technology will prove to be the economic salvation for Britain.

At the present time British industry is relatively uncompetitive. To 'catch up' with our competitors in the basic post-war industries will need immense investment and will almost certainly be a traumatic experience in social terms. However, it is now becoming clear that the microprocessor will render much of capital equipment and designs, both of our own and of our competitors, obsolete. If no one was to use the new technology it would not really matter, but Japan, West Germany, South Korea and the U.S.A. are already doing so in some measure. To remain competitive Britain and all its other competitors will have to do so too. Which means that the distance that Britain has fallen behind is irrelevant. If many machines all over the world have to be replaced it does not matter how old the previous machines were, for the cost, except in accountancy depreciation terms, remains constant. Thus the rules of the game have been changed and changed at a time and in a way which favour Britain.

To adopt the new techniques, buy the new machinery and

redesign the products requires capital and North Sea oil makes this available to the public sector and purse. However, the problem remains of capital investment for the private sector. The Wilson Committee on the Financial Institutions so far has received roughly 2 cwt of written evidence. Of this all but about two stone is claiming loudly and clearly that capital is sloshing in the gunwales of the City but no one wants it. Money may be sloshing around, but while many small, technologically oriented companies are desperate for money, the City will not help. Budding entrepreneurs have to turn to the British government agencies, U.S.A. or to the OPEC countries for finance. Large companies probably do use their profits for investment to the extent of about 70 per cent of all undertaken, but they rarely move into high-risk areas, preferring to buy in their expertise and products after the development stage by means of total or partial take-overs.

Why though is there a shortage of risk or venture capital in Britain? It is a crucial question, in that the microprocessor-based computing and systems industry and its services is at least one growth area with considerable export potential. The answer probably lies in the type of financial system that has evolved in Britain. New, small, high technology companies obviously cannot use retained profits as do large established companies. The need for finance is all the greater because development costs are often very high and money is needed to finance the considerable time lag between the inception of the company and the sale of any new product. Whilst it is feasible for large existing companies to incorporate the new technology in the production processes or the product itself, or in its offices, it is unlikely that such a company would be able itself to develop such techniques. A case in point is the giant General Electric Company who have moved into a joint venture with an existing producer – Fairchild – rather than taking the development further themselves.

Small companies, especially in their formative stages, have traditionally had finance problems. In high technology areas this problem is more acute as substantial sums of money are required and the period before returns are made is often long and indefinable. When confronted with a choice between this type of loan and a more traditional small business, the average

67

bank manager will unhesitatingly plump for the fish and chip shop. This is not the fault of the manager, who is not equipped to evaluate risk capital loans of this type, but of the system which provides for little alternative. The two largest savings institutions in Britain are the pension funds and insurance companies, pension funds now being the greater. Both place most of their funds in the Stock Exchange, gilts or equities, and property. Most of the dealings in the Exchange are just interchanging bits of paper, one insurance company buying someone else's shares or selling its own and not one halfpenny of this money ever reaches a company. This 'secondary market' accounts for about 90 per cent of share transactions and actual investment only occurs with the residual 10 per cent of new or rights issues. The innovator company is unlikely to be publicly quoted or to be seeking a quotation and thus despite even the generality of the above argument finds itself in an even worse position. Apart from a miniscule percentage of their funds set aside for the purpose, neither pension funds nor insurance companies make direct investments in enterprises. Such companies are therefore unable to take advantage of the monies, which are, by common consent, readily available for less risky purposes. There do exist some specialist funding agencies like the National Research Development Corporation, the I.C.F.C., Department of Industry and the National Enterprise Board, but having access to such is still immensely difficult.

For Britain this gap between companies and capital investment is doubly worrying because competitor countries benefit from mechanisms which cater precisely for this problem. In the United States the Government spends billions of dollars as a procurer of research and in certain defence industries Congress has decreed a total 'buy American' policy. If this fails, or the money is spread too thinly then there are risk capital specialists who will not only provide adequate money but, understanding the fundamental problems, provide the management and marketing expertise. In America finance and technology actually meet on an amicable basis and converse in a common language.

West Germany, Japan and France all have a different approach. In these countries, directly and indirectly, the government provides finance or services to private industry for research and development. In Japan it is estimated that £500 billion has already been spent on applied electronic research and in Germany around £300 million. These countries also develop government laboratories on a customer or client relationship with industry to remove pressure from the cash flow of companies, whether large or small. None (France apart) maintain large armament industries to provide orders but compensate for this in these other ways. These are more effective because the research or finance is put to applied uses and in Japan this is heavily biased towards the actual techniques of production, thus increasing efficiency and productivity.

One final point has to be made about the British system. The Stock Exchange thrives on the movement of share prices. Static prices, however high, mean that no dealings are taking place, which in turn means no commission for brokers and jobbers. It is thus in the interest of the Stock Exchange participants (though not the quoted companies) to 'talk up' or 'talk down' shares. The favourite method of doing this is to predict a profit for a company which, if it is then exceeded or reduced in the published returns, affects the share price. To maintain a steady series of movements the annual profit statement has now been replaced by half-yearly and even quarterly statements. Whilst this leads to share movements it also means that the approach taken by not only brokers but the financial institutions and the residual personal investor to savings and investment is becoming increasingly short term. The moment a company starts to reduce its profits, change its P/E ratio adversely and become more highly geared, the institutions take fright. They may not sell, they may set up a protection committee – known as either an Investors Protection Committee or a Shareholders Protection Committee – and put pressure on senior management to put their house in order i.e. re-achieve their profitability. Whilst this sounds laudable it unfortunately militates against investments in developments which are either uncertain or have a long gestation period.

This short-term approach, though not excusable, is firmly rooted traditional British financial caution. The institutions must, by definition, be conservative. Insurance companies have to guarantee the possible payments consequent upon disasters to their policy holders. Pension funds have to guarantee the

69

incomes of retired people. Banks have to guarantee their clients their money back at short notice if they wish to withdraw their deposits. All three major institutions must thus have their policies dictated by prudence and although this has worked to the advantage of the reputation of British institutions it militates against present day investment needs – and technological advances.

The system is defended, not surprisingly, by the participants on the grounds that it allocates finances in an optional manner and furthermore has been tried and tested for two centuries. The historic argument is a symptom of precisely the 'conservatism' which is most inhibiting. The institutions do not appear to have realized that the world is changing or that it is the systems within which they work, rather than their judgements, which are being criticized. The other defence is more fundamental for it confuses the allocation of resources with the allocation of finance.

Finance is but one resource amongst many. Skills, expertise, the whole of manpower and work, land, weather, natural materials are all resources which play a major part in any productive process. It does not follow that if you allocate finances optimally, that is to get the highest return consistent with risk, then the allocation of resources will inevitably follow in a similarly optimal manner. The property boom of the late 1960s is an example of this; would anyone claim that this represented a 'best situation'? An economic system also displays many structural rigidities: a lack of competition, large oligopolistic firms, transnational corporations, government policies and lack of mobility are just some of them. These tend to mean that the theory of the market allocation of finance will never correspond to reality and that as technology develops this gap will increase.

Microprocessors are thus coming into operation in a world which is suffering from its greatest depression since the 1930s. One thing that is certain as the present decade comes to a close is that there is much spare capacity and many under-used or non-used resources. The new techniques will enable producers of both goods and services to provide the same existing levels of production while employing even fewer resources. The trick of course will be to increase the demand for products of all descriptions, while boosting growth by at least 5 per cent to reduce unemployment. Perhaps the equation may be impossible.

In the short term the world picture is not encouraging. But strange as it may seem, for Britain the possible outcome is far more optimistic. So poorly has the British economy been performing, so run down the industrial structure, and so dramatic is likely to be the impact of North Sea oil, that there is a very real chance, given the right policies, that Britain could challenge her competitors. If we perform the British economic miracle it will have to be based on the new technologies using the breathing space afforded by oil.

6 Unemployment and the long term

The shadow of large-scale long-term unemployment is hovering over the Western world and is starting to worry more than just unions, a few prominent politicians and bankers. What was supposed to be a short sharp recession which would give time to cope with the inflation following the oil price rises, is turning into a longer and no longer welcome slump. Social security and other payments have thus far played their part in a very subdued reaction to the phenomenon, but for how long will this be the case?

Unemployment is very difficult to define, although commonsense would suggest otherwise, since every jobless person knows that he is jobless. The difficulties arise in trying to record all the people who are unemployed and then, for statistical purposes, exactly defining the total workforce so as to look at percentage changes. Each country has its own method of computing the figures and political expediency unfortunately plays its part in definition and collation so that some data are very unreliable. The social situation also distorts the figures. For example a country with a very large percentage of land workers will have artificially low unemployment rates as many people doing no full time productive work in family groups are counted as working in the family. The O.E.C.D. recognizes this problem and has standardized unemployment figures to attempt to adjust for these discrepancies.

Britain officially has around 1·5 million people unemployed including school leavers. To be more accurate this should be rephrased as 1·5 million formally seeking jobs through the Department of Employment system. Clearly some people will use other methods. People 'sign-on' at labour exchanges so as to receive their unemployment pay and these are counted as unemployed. But some people don't get unemployment benefit – some married women, for example, so they don't 'sign on' and their lack of work goes unrecorded. It is little different in principle to the rural society undercounting. Since Britain has the largest percentage of women in this category of all the O.E.C.D. countries and given the Equal Opportunities Commission and its effect, this percentage should increase, and thus the gap between the official statistics and reality widens, and will continue to widen.

At the time that official British statistics were suggesting 1·5 million unemployed the O.E.C.D. adjusted figures were showing Britain to have 2·1 million or 8·1 per cent of the workforce out of work – the highest percentage in the O.E.C.D. The *A.S.T.M.S. Quarterly Economic Review* has been using these adjusted figures for the past three years and getting public disavowals and sometimes gentle abuse for doing so. But the O.E.C.D. have now legitimized this approach.

Whilst it is only too true in present circumstances to say that those people out of a job don't really care why, economists care a lot. They have tried to categorize unemployment and labelled the various types, but the problem remains to subdivide the unemployed accurately into these particular types. 'Frictional' unemployment is that caused when people change jobs. They often leave, sign on and then get a job within a few weeks. It is short-term and does not constitute any major problem, indeed it is inevitable for so long as people change their employment. Structural unemployment is long-term and as its name suggests, is part and parcel of the structure of the economy or industry. There is also a new concept 'The natural level of unemployment' – a monetarist concept to describe those *unnaturally* made unemployed by government economic policies aimed at maintaining a stability of the growth of money supply. The only importance that can be attached to such definitions is that, if correctly identified, different causes of unemployment can be combated by different policies if any action, of course, is thought to be desirable. Finally, there is 'technological' unemployment, a concept used in France on an official level. This is unemployment which has been directly caused by the introduction of new technology and is used to determine whether or not people can get the special redundancy compensation which accrues to such circumstances.

But life, especially economic life, declines to remain within easily defined categories. For example, there are at present too many ships in the world for the level of current trade. One result is that most shipyards, in most countries, are working well below capacity and several thousands of potential workers, or former workers are unemployed. The question is, are they unemployed because of the level of demand for ships, or does it go deeper than this? If world demand recovers, then will the shipwrights of north-east England get their jobs back, given that a lack of investment over the past 50 years has made them hopelessly uncompetitive compared with either Japan or South Korea? Are they really technologically unemployed, but with the technology being applied in another country? Will steel plants ever need to recruit labour again, especially if motor manufacturers switch to lighter plastic bodies to conserve fuel? If so, it is a somewhat different picture to that of just waiting for demand for steel to revive on the assumption it will always be used for the same purposes as before.

What may start out as a slightly longer period of frictional unemployment originating in a depression can well turn into structural unemployment stemming from all manner of changes which relate to technological change. The product itself can be superseded, overseas technology might well make an industry over-productive, technology in a purchaser industry might have changed. In a period of low technological change this is not an important issue; in a period of fast technological change and thus uncertainty these factors assume a fundamental importance.

Gross unemployment figures, although showing the overall position and trend in a country, hide a multitude of differences. Unemployment levels may not only differ regionally in Britain, but within the regions themselves there are huge disparities. In Britain, certain regions have traditionally suffered higher unemployment levels than others; Scotland and Clydeside in particular, the north-east and the north-west, all with a preponderance of heavy industry have endured the highest levels. The south-east and London have had the lowest levels, yet in parts of London like the East End with over $\frac{3}{4}$ million workers in all, the percentage of unemployment is actually higher than in Scotland. If this is broken down even further into sections of London boroughs (most of which have populations far greater than the average town), unemployment is even higher. These geographical imbalances especially around city centres make the drawing up of overall employment policy a tricky task, and really argue for more refined methods of economic planning and policy. Such intra-regional differences become even more significant when new technologies arrive, as they may have the effect of either reinforcing or distorting existing demographic trends. This pattern is even more complex when it is realized that even within high unemployment areas there are vacancies for some jobs, most often skilled, such as toolmakers, secretarial staff or computer people.

In Western Europe the Common Market has itself had a marked effect on the distribution of unemployment. The Market is physically large and the areas on the periphery, notably Scotland, Southern Italy, Brittany and south-west England have not fared as well as those nearest to the centre. There is a gravitational pull by the 'golden triangle' whereby resources are imploded into the Brussels, Ruhr, Amsterdam, Paris ambit. This not only makes much of Britain peculiarly vulnerable to periods of short-term economic depression, but it worsens the potential problems when and if work methods and the consequent resource allocations change.

Although the E.E.C. regional policy was set up to counter this known shift, its effect has been disappointingly marginal, especially in the United Kingdom. Six thousand two hundred million units of account (M.U.A.) were allocated to the Common Agricultural Policy in 1977, but only 500 M.U.A. to the Regional Fund, a discrepancy which, in itself, points to E.E.C. priorities. This pales even further into insignificance if the regional fund payments to the U.K. are matched with U.K. total contributions – most of which go the Common Agricultural Policy to keep food prices high and further damage the U.K. balance of payments. However half-heartedly the E.E.C. is approaching this problem at present it will have to be totally committed to it in the future. Without such commitment the existence of the market itself will be threatened.

The U.K. and the E.E.C. are not alone in having city centre

and regional work problems. The United States has several pockets of very high unemployment amidst affluence, especially in city centres. This leads to a second point which is the racial imbalance of unemployment. In the U.S.A. the unemployment rate is 7·32 per cent but amongst black people it is 12·5 per cent and amongst black youths is even higher. The U.S. unions believe that unemployment is actually nearer 10 per cent and that black unemployment is nearer 20 per cent. The same phenomenon can be seen in Britain, especially in London areas, such as Hackney and Lambeth, and again it is the young black people who are the most affected. Whilst much of this has unfortunately to be put down to some employers' – and some employees' – bigotry and prejudice, some is a consequence of the poor educational systems in black areas or poor white and mixed areas. Technology change, especially one based on micro-electronics and a considerable amount of knowledge, may make this lack of educational attainment an even more serious handicap.

The size of the labour force is not a stable factor either, but it is more predictable than other elements. Assuming that death and morbidity rates are roughly constant (or at a known rate of change) and that participation rates are constant (they are not) then the workforce depends on the birth rate from 16 to 21 years earlier. Despite these uncertainties and the legislative uncertainty of what the retirement age will be, predictions of the probable labour force in the future are more accurate than for almost any comparable estimation.

In round terms the number of extra workers in the U.K. entering the labour market up to 1991 is forecast as 2·5 million. This increase will be at its heaviest in the period up to 1986 and thereafter it will start to slow down. This is a peculiarly disturbing thought. If at present we cannot provide jobs for 1·5 million people, how will we cope with the extra 2·5 million? The Institute of Manpower Studies at the University of Sussex has done some work on these figures and indeed appears to justify the current climate of pessimism in Britain.

Their analysis is quite simple. Totally disregarding technological change, it treats growth of Gross Domestic Product as having the same employment implications as it has had in the past. The future manpower levels were determined first. Their various growth rates of Gross Domestic Product (a measure of the total work done in a country) are assessed as an average for the years up to 1991. The trend size of the labour force is then compared with the trend of jobs available which are derived from the growth rate with the assumption just noted. Two sets of results have been published. The first was *The Times* newspaper articles of 15 May 1978, postulating an average growth rate of 2·75 per cent over the 13 years and an increase in output per head of 2·54 per cent average. Whilst not impossible to achieve, it suggests that these would imply a 'healthy economic future'. The overall job gap was 11·9 per cent or 3·38 million.

Within this there were, however, some very interesting shifts. The unemployment rise slowed over the last five years as by 1986 the estimate was for 2·9+million. Secondly, unemployment amongst males was estimated to be 16·5 per cent and females 5·4 per cent. The age distribution of unemployment was unequally shared. Over one in five of those under 20 would be unemployed down to one in ten of the 25–54 (the prime of life) age group. One other important point is that the study predicts that the number of men employed will continue to decline and the number of women employed will continue to increase by over 100,000 per year. The final important point was that there would be marked changes in unemployment by sector, with the greatest numbers in the secondary and unclassified sectors (the non-manufacturing, service sectors).

The second study (the first in time) done by this unit was for a B.B.C./TV special on the future of employment. It assumed four different rates of growth, with a single projection for the labour force. Productivity growth was again reckoned to be directly related to the rate of growth of the economy and somehow homogeneous as to job content. It also assumed that technical change was related to past trends in its relationship to productivity – in other words, it is assumed to be neutral. The results were dramatic. For an average of 3·5 per cent growth over the 25 years, unemployment would be a mere 418,000 in 1991; 3 per cent growth 2·5 million; 2·5 per cent growth 4·78 million and 2 per cent growth 6·78 million. Whilst this assumes unchanged government policies, it does show the arithmetical dependence of unemployment on the rate of G.D.P. growth.

The Cambridge Economic Policy Group (C.E.P.G., one of the most prestigious economic forecasting units in the world) has disturbingly arrived at roughly the same figure, but through a totally different mechanism. The Group employs more orthodox forecasting techniques using Britain's only medium-term economic model, which itself is based on Keynesian orthodoxies and the normal parameters. When attempting to forecast anything, especially in economics, the assumptions that are made determine the ultimate prediction. The longer the time-scale over which the analysis is made, the more tenuous the assumptions become and thus more possible errors can creep in. The most basic assumption made by the C.E.P.G. is to assume unchanged government policies. These are broadly categorized as 'orthodox policies' and consist of tight fiscal (tax) control and restraint of wages, both of which will be designed to reduce the rate of inflation and to aid the balance of payments, thus retaining a higher parity of sterling with foreign currencies. Measures to combat any rising unemployment will continue to be palliative rather than fundamental and measures acting on the supply side will be the continuation of the tripartite discussions under the 'industrial strategy'. This involves the discussion held under the aegis of the National Economic Development Office, the Sector Working Parties and the broad policies and targets which they are formulating.

Whether these assumptions are realistic is open to question. Could any government stand by and see registered unemployment rise to over 10 per cent in the particular social circumstances of the 1970s? It does seem unlikely. However, as a projection of what would happen if policies do not change, the C.E.P.G. forecast represents a major and compelling piece of evidence and a strong stimulus to change.

The other main assumptions are that world trade will continue to be depressed and that import penetration in the U.K. will conform to previous relationships. Commodity prices are assumed to be constant relative to the price of manufacture with the exception of oil which will relatively rise from 1980 onward. Given these 'orthodox' policies, and the other assumptions, they estimate that the future growth of G.D.P. will be below 3 per cent up to 1980, below 2 per cent in the early 1980s and zero by the end of the 1980s. The reason for this slowdown will be the 'British disease' of a recurring balance of payments constraint. The C.E.P.G. assume that productivity will continue to grow at around 3 per cent per year over this period, although they do acknowledge that whilst this was true up to 1973, it has fallen since then. The assumptions of the probable labour supply are similar to those in the Institute of Manpower Studies analysis.

To reduce unemployment to 2 per cent (500,000) by 1990, the average rate of growth would have to be 4 per cent. In the U.K., we have never managed to grow at even 3·5 per cent for any three consecutive years since the war, let alone the twelve consecutive years needed. The slow growth projections by the Cambridge school would result in unemployment of 1·75 million in 1980, 3 million in 1985 and *4·5 million by 1990*.

These two sets of projections are not quite compatible. The Cambridge study takes an even dimmer view than the most pessimistic of the Sussex growth rates, yet its predicted level of unemployment is lower. If the Cambridge model is carried on to the end of the century, then unemployment figures of around 5 million would be expected.

What then can be made of these two dissimilar studies reaching approximately similar conclusions – certainly in the direction in which employment and jobs will move? The number of jobs needed to be created by the economy merely to prevent unemployment rising will be in the region of 2·5 million. This is the first and probably the most unpalatable truth. The second is that women will almost certainly be entering the labour force in ever increasing numbers, although it is almost certain that strenuous efforts will be made to prevent this from continuing. The third is that the growth rate of gross domestic product is crucial to the level of unemployment in the economy and the fact is that current government policies, indeed 'orthodox policies' will be helpless in the face of the probable circumstances.

The Cambridge argument specifically and overtly rejects the notion of 'technological unemployment' and the Sussex study implicitly rejects the concept. The Cambridge analysts in fact go further; they argue that technological unemployment did not really occur in the past, and given adequate policies will not do so in the future. To some extent, this is justifiable, if only in academic terms as it is always possible to think of political initiatives to employ people; but in the real world this has rarely been the case. There are fewer farriers and wagon-wheel makers today because their replacements were making new products – the car, the bus and the train; technology in this instance acted as a product. Let us suppose, however, that instead of supplanting the horse and carriage with alternative methods of transport, a new and improved method of making carriages and shoeing horses had been developed. The jobs would have been lost, but no demand, other than the limited use stimulated by cheaper carriages and maintenance, would have been available to re-employ people.

If, as we believe, recent events would show that growth in an economy does not automatically create jobs any more than does wealth automatically accrue to the country in which it is created, then the Sussex and Cambridge arguments based only upon growth are understated. If growth is not neutral with respect to jobs, but is likely to be increasingly destructive as far as work is concerned, then both sets of figures would have to be revised upwards. John Stuart Mill summed up this phenomenon succinctly in his adage 'the demand for commodities is not the demand for labour'. However, we believe that the studies' premises regarding underlying government policies and international policies are unlikely to be correct. In the short term, as unemployment grows, so governments will be forced into compensating actions, and up to the twenty-first century there will be many 'short terms'. However much this factor compensates for the underlying fundamental weaknesses of the British economy, we are equally convinced that technological unemployment will, if allowed to develop, rise over time to a high plateau.

The current short-term job creation schemes in most Western countries bear witness to the idea that governments are worried about unemployment rates, especially amongst the young. The current (mid-1978) estimate of the number of jobs created by these measures in the U.K. is 350,000. In the European Common Market, the same emphasis is being placed on 'keeping people busy'. There are various schemes in operation. The most favoured is to subsidize short-time working and Britain has had to change on to this method and away from its direct Temporary Employment Subsidy at the peremptory demand of the Common Market Commission. Job experience schemes and 'job swap' schemes are also popular in Europe, along with encouraging young people to stay in full-time education for as long as possible, so as to minimize formal unemployment. In both the E.E.C. and North America, unemployment amongst people under 20 is three times the average for all workers. Both sides of the Atlantic now seem set to increase the scope of schemes and to devote the necessary money. Britain plans to bring work contact or training to 250,000 young people after late 1978 and the U.S.A., whilst relying more on government jobs, will expand their schemes and attempt to have an effective monitoring mechanism. But these expedients can at best only be regarded as short-term and based on the premise that, sooner or later, unemployment will go away and the schemes will then be run down. As a British agency official involved in the job creation scheme programme laconically remarked 'it's like trying to shovel the tide back'.

The whole world is not suffering from a lack of jobs or young unemployment. The Eastern European bloc has managed to keep unemployment to a fractional minimum as a result of deliberate policy objectives. The right to work is written into the constitution of the Soviet Union and thus policies to make this possible are the prime objective rather than, as in the West, providing policies to reduce inflation and treating employment as the residual, and expendable parameter. Three factors contribute to making this difference workable in Eastern Europe. The first is the lower birth rate and thereby smaller rate of increase in the labour force. The second and third are, however, politically based.

The Comecon countries have one factor common to each of them. They can and do make the production (supply) side of the economy as responsive to political decisions as the demand side. This means that they can deliberately overman certain industries and deliberately reduce productivity so as to employ more people. For example, in Czechoslovakia industry uses roughly 20 per cent more workers for the same type of output and products than Western equivalents. In the trade-off between efficiency or productivity and work, work has won. This leads to strange labour-creating situations. A multi-storey hotel was built with 'magic eye' automatic door opening mechanisms, yet this hotel has a lady sitting near the lift door with a converted table-tennis bat which she waves in front of the beam in the event of people approaching. Is it better, one asks, to run a society in a deliberately inefficient way to provide work for all or is it better to have an efficient society, down-grading the importance of work and distributing the profits from that work more equitably?

A centralized and publicly owned system can work clearly in either way and the path followed depends on political directives. The essential dilemma for the West is that by and large the supply side of industry cannot be controlled in this way, or at least previous attempts to do so have failed and cajolery and coercion have not proved successful. Without a degree, or several degrees of control, these options are not really open. The important part is not the centralization – that is as irrelevant to the argument as stating that all companies should be the same size as Exxon – it is the control of output, productivity and return. There is now evidence that the Comecon countries have realized this, and are attempting to decentralize, introduce a market element and, indeed, start to improve efficiency. This has to be seen against the move to open their economies to imports – inefficiency only survives in a long-term closed economy.

The long-term prospects in the West are decidedly gloomy when viewed against the current ethos of a need to work. Both on an international basis and a parochial U.K. basis, the chances of sustained growth sufficient to remove unemployment are very limited. Yet all the analyses specifically discount technology and assume that growth in the future will have the same productivity impact and thus the same employment impact as in past years. We shall now look at technological changes in more detail and demonstrate that this may be a pious hope. For each spurt of growth based on traditional patterns and the new technological devices at hand will actually decrease the employment possibilities overall and in some sectors in particular. The corollary of this is that it may, if attitudes do not change and suitable mechanisms are not introduced, be better to become inefficient and work on the Comecon pattern. Such a counsel is, however, one of defeatism and conservatism. A better life for all is possible – through concerted political action.

7 The work impact – so far

One of the principal defects in British statistic gathering is that we do not have any valuable overall analysis of changes in technology and their work effects. Britain is not alone in this respect, many countries select and collect their data in essentially old-fashioned modes. The major factor in this distressing state of affairs is that Keynes believed in demand management and the main thrust of statistical collection and analysis is to get enough information to put such policies into practice. The supply side, be it productive, distributive or service, has been relatively neglected on the grounds that such data was without a practical spin-off. Not only are the available figures insufficient, they are frequently out of date and inadequately classified. If all that were needed was to adjust demand there would be little difficulty, but once some form of intervention on the supply side is thought desirable it now has to be done either on a one-off basis or by floundering around in the statistical dark.

World industrial strategies are now so integrated as to make the old-fashioned classifications a mockery in terms of the traditional company. What is worse is that they become totally irrelevant in process, skill and employment terms; even now there are transcending systems which make the production of heavy billets and delicate scientific apparatus very similar. It is this integration that makes the possibility of major work changes consequent upon a major technological breakthrough that much more likely.

The microprocessor or silicon chip, the impulse behind the new technology, varies in power, uses, costs and ability. The simple 4K chips used in TV games, simple watches and calculators now cost less than £1 each. 4K simply means that the chip is capable of 'memorizing' 4,000 bytes. A byte is either an eight or sixteen form of computer word. The prime object in the production of chips has been to mass produce at a reasonable cost, elements with increasingly large memory systems. The National Enterprise Board company, Inmos, will be (it is hoped) manufacturing a 64K chip with sixteen times the memory of the simple one. This does not mean that it will be sixteen times as effective or have sixteen times the number of uses, but obviously its increased potential allows it to be used for more sophisticated purposes across a greater range. The major competitors to Inmos will be Mostek, Intel, Texas Instruments, Motorola Signetics and I.T.T. from the U.S.A.: Hitachi, Toshiba and Nippon Electric from Japan, and G.E.C./Fairchild on a U.K./U.S.A. basis and a yet un-named French company. Clearly it is not an easy field to enter, but as has been argued, it is vital that we do so.

Computers have always been the most awesome types of new tool. Whilst other tools have been developed to replace muscle power the computer and its adjuncts were the first to replace brain power. What a big main frame computer can now perform by way of analysis of circumstances which leads to almost instant decisions on the fastest, safest or cheapest way to perform a task, the microprocessor, so most experts believe, will be able to carry out shortly or perhaps in five years time. Strategic planners realise this and consequently wish Britain to have its own production capabilities since political and trade groupings have historically had a habit of shifting and so supplies could be at risk. The French had the same possibilities in mind when they, too, decided to move into the manufacturing business. For the 1980s it could spell disaster, industrial, commercial, if a regular supply of this new raw material (the microprocessor) cannot be guaranteed.

Behind all this reasoning is the underlying assumption that microprocessors will not only be used, but will be intensively used. Reinforcing this view is the Department of Industry's decision to spend £15 million on encouraging their use. In addition to this small spur the announcement by the Prime Minister that the Government will make £200 million available for the training of people and subsidies for companies which use the new technology shows that it is being taken very seriously indeed. And yet, there must be some doubt as to how quickly Britain will or can start to use the new technology. A superficial inspection, and that is really all our statistics allow us, would suggest that Britain is lagging well behind the U.S.A., Japan, Germany, France, South Korea, Canada, Switzerland and Holland in the application of microprocessors. Even more serious is the evidence suggesting that neither the interest nor the expertise is present either. Department of Industry surveys have shown that less than 50 per cent of British companies realize the potential of micro-chips and only 5 per cent have taken any action. These survey results would tend to confirm the widely held views of both domestic and foreign critics that the failings of British industry have to be laid fairly and squarely at the door of domestic managements. Such managements would appear to be displaying their traditional conservative, blinkered and amateur approach whilst our competitors pursue their vigorously rational aims. If our international competitors are using microprocessors, then unless Britain erects permanent trade barriers, it is clear that we shall have to do so too. If microprocessor technology is the instrument by which British industry will finally extricate itself from its poor competitive position, then it is too sensitive an instrument to be left entirely in the hands of the current wave of British managements – unions will have to provide the thrust and drive.

From the areas and one or two examples of applications of microprocessors, let us now turn to the problem of trying to set down some criteria as to the areas in which they will be used. By definition these will be based on functions and processes, not on industrial classifications. This is the common factor linking the revolutionary steam and electric engines and micro-electronics; the inter-sectoral and multi-use capability. Whilst the original industrial sectors were based on separate technologies and skills, these have not been shared between sectors so that the sectors themselves become merely names rather than unique processes. We can divide these rules or characteristics into two sections: those which affect processes and those that affect products.

One key characteristic is the microprocessor's ability to respond to situations faster than humans can possibly react; another its manner of working in an environment hostile to the health of human beings. A third major characteristic is its ability to diagnose problems, providing these fall into a pre-determined and thus a programmable range; this is clearly true about most machine breakdowns. Furthermore, if the response needed to this diagnosis is programmable in advance too, the microprocessor can do this job as well.

When these processes are required frequently or continuously, microprocessors are now being used for the entire sequence. When a given set of tasks is repetitive or predictably changing, microprocessors are being adopted or where time is of the essence in communications, either written or oral, microprocessor technology is being used. Where the system is susceptible to interference which may have undesirable results, microprocessors are being used to avoid it.

The product itself, however, is as susceptible to change as is the process of manufacturing it, and in the longer term probably has more work change effects associated with it than the method of its production. Electro-mechanical control, sequence and other systems at present used in mass-produced products, will be replaced by micro-electronics. Products where cheapness, miniaturization, durability or reliability are important for marketing purposes will incorporate micro-processors. Products which use or could use logic systems and products which can be attached to other products (for example, TV games or telephone message receivers) will all become dependent on microprocessors.

Finally, there are those products made by small batch control rather than mass production methods; where these have specialist control systems which can be replaced by programmable chips then that will occur. As we shall see later, the above are two comprehensible if rather 'dry' lists which have, on analysis, an enormous number of repercussions for work and work processes.

Philips of Eindhoven, a company which employs nearly half a million people on a world-wide basis, is engaged in electrical manufacturing. The company has estimated that even allowing for a 3 per cent annual growth rate in turnover over 10 years, by the end of that period it will be 56 per cent overmanned. This results almost entirely from the combination of new assembly and production methods and a vast simplification in each individual product, a few of which will be new in market terms. The change is substantially due to the replacement of existing electro-mechanical systems with microprocessor systems. The work is mainly light batch assembly and what applies to electrical production also applies to other industries using the same methods and producing products capable of being correspondingly simplified. Mass production techniques are always ripe for this type of development.

How does the microprocessor actually produce this 'disemployment'? Assembly work is, despite the equipment needed, basically and heavily labour intensive. The development of a production system is in several stages and these have been worked through by Chris Freeman and Ray Curnow at S.P.R.U. of Sussex University in their 'diagnostic triangle'. At the base is the collection and preparing of component blanks. These are then fabricated into components by milling, machinery, etc, and then assembled into sub-systems. The sub-systems are subsequently assembled into a system and finally the product has to be tested, sold, installed and maintained with all the working infrastructure that this entails. On top of the pyramid are the design and innovative teams and linking the pyramid together by a form of skeleton are the managerial teams. Any company which undertook all of these functions would be unusually integrated on a 'vertical' pattern. More often a company will specialize in component manufacture, or in assembly, or in servicing a producer. There will thus be many companies which could be affected by such a change in the design or production method of just one product.

The microprocessor tears the heart out of the pyramid, leaving the shell behind. From the outside the company looks the same, has the same name and produces the same sort of products, but in fact this is an illusion behind which lies the reality of grave disemployment. The microprocessor allows for a one-shot integrated manufacturing process; consequently the system or sub-system has been integrated on to one or more silicon chips, while the fabrication, the assembly, the indirect stores etc, have often been eliminated.

One major result of this is now becoming apparent, especially in the industries which are horizontally integrated, like automobile manufacturing. Company boundaries are being blurred and work is gravitating towards those companies which produce the microprocessors. This is a function of the design systems which need an expertise in the new technologies which the traditional suppliers cannot, or have not been willing, to provide. In the U.S.A. both Intel and Motorola are designing and now manufacturing sub-systems for automobiles, which are having a deleterious effect on the traditional suppliers. It also means that the design of new automobiles can only be undertaken either after deep consultation with microprocessor producers, or even by those producers themselves. In Britain companies like Lucas or Smiths Industries will have to acquire the new capabilities quickly, or end up with a truncated business.

Let us now look at an average company, vertically integrated, in the manufacturing sector. By average, we mean in *The Times* top 200 companies and with 20,000 or so employees. *Though it should be borne in mind that only 10 per cent of the British labour force is actively and fully involved in any direct manufacturing process.* Even in manufacturing companies the Eltis and Bacon drift towards indirect jobs has been working. Along comes the microprocessor and significant changes rapidly begin to show themselves.

The design of the product itself alters. The number of components is reduced by, let us say, one-third, a reasonable enough assumption in the light of present practice, although perhaps a conservative one over the longer run. The number of sub-assembled systems is correspondingly reduced and the final assembly process thereby simplified. Testing and maintenance become much easier and even self-diagnostic. Each of these simplifications must mean that at each stage less labour is required. But also less stocks need to be held because there are fewer and more reliable components, so that warehouse and stock control staffs become redundant. The volume of internal invoicing, billings and transferring are also reduced along with associated staff, so that clerical, administrative, managerial and transport workers are also made redundant. Because the new components will be microprocessor designed, there will probably be a reduction in designers, draughtsmen and engineers. Also since the new components will be smaller, less warehouse space will be needed, thus affecting the manning of construction teams; likewise with smaller size office blocks so fewer office workers will be required, and again fewer transport workers will be needed as a given truck or wagon load will take in more components than before. All of which happens when the design is changed.

It is highly probable, however, that this will not be the only change instituted by the company. Changes in the methods of production, partly brought about by the component changes and partly by more efficient techniques, will also be introduced. Robotics in all their various forms are starting to come into operation and to be sold in standard forms. The components themselves will be standardized and almost certainly be made interchangeable across models and product lines. Packaging becomes easier as products become smaller and the packaging process itself now becomes automated. Warehousing and stock control is a prime target for computerization as is the optimum manner of materials handling, an area where jobs are already being lost. The clerical staff will be using word processors, electronic typewriters and filing, whilst the communications system will be revolutionized on an internal basis by using a combination of micro-computers, word processors and tele-phones. Just by keeping up with and embracing the new known technologies this selected but average firm could cut its labour force by around 50 per cent. If one firm in a sector does this successfully and reduces its costs concurrently with producing a more reliable product, other firms in that sector will either have to copy it or see their market share eroded.

One example of this sequence is in the decline of British television set manufacture. Britain has been suffering from an excess of imported television sets from Japan and television tubes and other components from the Far East. The imported sets are cheaper, more reliable and unfortunately sometimes of a higher technical standard and quality. The British manufac-turers either had to copy the Japanese systems or go out of business altogether, and certainly the competition has reduced the numbers employed in Britain quite dramatically. Thorn Electrical Industries decided to adopt Japanese methods and the result has been a 50 per cent cut in assembly plant staffing for the same level of output – to take place over a phased period. Thorn's and the unions represented there were confronted with a choice: either use the new technology or become immobilized and see the firm totally disappear from the colour TV set sector. If the second choice had been made it would have only been a short time before such sets were built in Germany or Eire and even if the U.K. Government kept out Japanese sets, it could not refuse entry to E.E.C.-manufactured sets. This pattern of choice will be discussed later in the book, but it is certain that the TV manufacturing dilemma will be repeated many times in different industries in the future. It is also instructive to look at precisely what the Japanese TV manufacturers have managed to do since 1970.

In components terms in 1970, the average 20 inch colour set contained two integrated circuits: by 1977 it had four integrated circuits. These replaced or made redundant components in the following volumes: almost a 100 per cent reduction in transistors down to thirty-four, an 80 per cent reduction in diodes down to thirty-eight, and about 80 per cent reduction in other parts. As an added bonus the amount of electricity consumption was decreased in the new sets from 155 watts to 85 watts: a saving passed on to the consumer in lower electricity bills.

The number of employees has, in consequence of this and more efficient and computer controlled production lines, been cut. In 1972 Hitachi employed 9000 on colour TV production, in 1976 this was down to 4300; the story is similar with other large manufacturers. National Panasonic's workforce fell from 9875 to 3900 and Sony from 4498 to 2278. In all, the big seven Japanese colour TV producers almost halved their labour force from nearly 48,000 to 25,000. In this same period, the number of TV sets manufactured *rose* by 25 per cent from 8·4 million sets in 1972 to 10·5 million sets in 1976. This increase in productivity could not possibly be achieved by workers working harder or by exhortation. It has been achieved by an immense investment in product and process design in an area where Britain has an appalling record.

TV set manufacture is interesting in a different context. Back in 1965 both the B.B.C. and I.T.V. were asked for their projections on the number of colour TV sets that would be in operation in Britain by 1975. The B.B.C. estimated 750,000 and the I.T.V. 2 million, and were worried that figures appeared unduly high. In fact there were 8 million sets in the U.K. by this date. We only mention this to show that the British consistently underestimate the impact of new technologies and the speed with which they will take effect. TV is but one example of where integrated circuits have led to a collapse of work. There are others, both currently in operation and pending.

We have examined the watch industry in an earlier chapter and noted that the cash register industry went along the same road. A 1977 statement by National Cash Register, the company that was nearly 'wiped out' through misreading the electronic revolution (but later recovered by joining it) stated, 'The electronic products that we are manufacturing today . . . have a labour content of about 25 per cent of their predecessors. Today the manufacturing operation primarily involves the assembly of purchased components . . . our total employment in manufacturing plants is down to 18,000 compared with 37,000 in 1970.' The same dilemma exists as was evident in British TV manufacturing; the successful company needs fewer workers, whereas the unsuccessful ones go to the wall. The Dundee operation of N.C.R. points to the future. At one time it employed 6000 workers in eight plants. By mid-1975 there were 3000 workers in four plants. Earlier this year further redundancies were announced and despite union opposition and action substantially diminishing the number, some will still go ahead. The Chairman stated *inter alia* that the redundancies were caused by various factors, including the technological simplification of the 8010 family micro-computers and the microprocessors which drive them. In addition he stated: 'As our products become more technically advanced, their labour content tends to decline', and added that *no* computer company is in a position to pledge stability of labour requirements. All these statements should be looked upon as a sign of the future and the Chairman congratulated on his honesty.

In this area, both firms which missed the switch to electronics and those which took part, have folded amid the new intense market competition. A division of the U.S. giant Pitney-Bowes lost at least £20 million and withdrew; M.S.I., another U.S. firm, and Bunker-Ramo, yet another, both left the market. The business machine division of Singer was put up for sale after a £10 million loss despite having 60 per cent of the U.S. point-of-sale market. Anker-Werke, a German firm, which continued to make electro-mechanical equipment went bankrupt in 1977 and Gross Cash Registers of the U.K. had to be taken over by Chubb to avoid the same fate. This new intense competition, so evident in watch and calculator manufacturing, is a symptom of the first productive flush of new technologies and has a marked destabilizing influence. In time, however, the situation will settle down with the dominant companies taking the lion's share of the market. They will, however, be the most efficient and, in this context, almost certainly employ the fewest people. Which is not intended to apply to cash registers or point-of-sale computers alone, but also to other areas where dynamic changes can take place as, for example, aircraft or automobile instrumentation.

The changes on the manufacturing side of TV and point-of-sale equipment carry serious effects for other secondary work. In TV the major area is that of servicing. This now becomes much easier and faster, and fewer people will be needed to carry out the same volume of service, whilst the sets themselves should be more reliable. This is all due basically to the integrated nature of the parts. Where in the past there would have to be extensive testing, soldering, re-wiring etc, a defective set assembly is removed after simple diagnostic tests and replaced with a new one, which just slips in. What may be encouraging for TV repairmen is the fact that there is patently a need for more of them, given the present time taken for response after complaint and this may, as in other similar cases, lead to a better service for no extra cost and no additional unemployment.

The effect of the transition from electro-mechanical cash registers to computer terminal registers is different in both kind and degree. The potential of these instruments in the large establishments is very considerable in relation to jobs. They can link with other terminals automatically to produce daily and even hourly stock control statements and automatically order from warehouses when pre-decided critically low levels of goods are reached. In the U.S.A. the totally automated super-market has now reached the suburbs of some cities. Goods are stamped with magnetic price codes, the shopper selects, takes the goods to the check-out device which reads the prices, delivers the bill (a credit card payment is automatically checked), pays and leaves the shop. The only people needed at present are shelf-stackers, and even there the new generation of forklift equipment might make them redundant. In the U.K. we have not developed to this extent or perhaps as the authors believe, we will never willingly submit to such a dehumanizing system. Nevertheless the stock and warehouse control, as well as experiments with magnetic pricing codes are now in operation and for retail trade assistants the future is correspondingly limited.

Already, in Chapter 4, we have mentioned the new 'System X' in the telecommunications industry. Mr Ken Corfield, the Managing Director of Standard Telephones and Cables (I.T.T.) and President of the Telecommunications Manufacturing Association, said in 1977 that the manufacturing process of System X would be 'almost that of a laboratory, eliminating the dirt, drudgery and physical work of current manufacturing with its stamping, pressing, turning, liquid soldering and labour intensive assembly.' At present there are the old electro-mechanical Cross-bar/Strowger exchanges, TXE4, a semi-electronic exchange system and the new electronic System X. For every 100 workers employed on producing Strowger equipment only forty are needed to produce TXE4 and a mere four are needed for System X. Whilst final levels should be higher than this, the American manufacturer, American Telephone and Telegraph (A.T. & T.) has reduced its labour force from 39,200 in 1970 to 18,500 in 1977, and it does argue that there will be a collapse of 'telecomm' manufacturing work. But the consequences go further. The new equipment is both more reliable and more easily serviced than the old so that a better service to consumers can be anticipated. But service engineers may well find they have no jobs. In the U.S.A., A.T. & T. have estimated that there will be a 75 per cent reduction in the number of persons needed to install, diagnose faults and repair the new system. The British Post Office Engineering Union has made its thoughts known loudly and clearly on this subject, and these and other union reactions will be discussed later.

The traditional main-frame big computer field is another which uses similar systems and techniques and, as in our previous examples, strangely enough is also threatening employment levels. Today I.B.M. makes ten times as many logic circuits as it

94

did in 1970, but with the same size labour force. In essence, computer manufacturing has been a labour intensive assembly process and thus the micro-circuitry has the same impact on production, storage and secondary jobs possibilities as on other similar assembly systems.

All the examples so far have been in broadly what might be described as electronic industries. In fact it is hardly surprising that these should lead in the application of micro-electronics. They are in the best position to recognize and evaluate new electronic advances and have the expertise on tap to develop and adapt to them. Their lead, however, is accidental and temporary. Other industries are starting to realize the value of the new system and incorporate either micro-circuitry in products or in production or other business methods.

The automobile industry is, we anticipate, on the brink of using them in the vehicles themselves. These micro-electronic controlled functions, as opposed to conventional ones, will cut down on the miles of conventional wiring systems used and yet again make the diagnosis of faults and servicing far easier. In the production of the sub-system, the system itself and the assembly into the vehicle, the tasks will be immensely simplified and the result will be far fewer jobs. Yet, there is a further reason why jobs will be lost and this is the change in the production process itself.

Industrial robots are a great disappointment to those who see such things only as humanoid form. They are functional, not at all aesthetically pleasing, but very efficient. They are used in an increasing number of industrial and other processes, from work in radio-active areas in nuclear installations, through TV and car production, up to defusing or exploding bombs in Ulster. In the automobile industry Britain is lagging far behind in new process techniques and this in turn has bearing on the relative attractiveness of foreign models in price (for a car including what are optional extras in the U.K.), style, reliability and finish.

Volkswagen in Germany use robots, for welding and body panel handling. They manufacture their own robots and in fact sell them as a commercial sideline. They can be rebuilt and reprogrammed and, in theory at least, three robots can replace ten men on a two shift system. Incidentally, robots do not strike and need no rest, but as Walter Reuther once shrewdly observed 'they don't buy cars' either. Whilst direct comparisons are often invidious V.W. produces twice British Leyland's target output, but employs only 80 per cent of British Leyland's workforce. Volvo, in its turn, has installed a body welding line manned by twenty-nine robots. This line was previously frequently stopped because the work was hard and tedious and absenteeism high, but now the seventy employees have been redeployed into more agreeable areas.

Fiat is using a new mobile multi-programmed Robogate line Only twenty-five men are needed to man it as against the previous 125, but to date Fiat have been forced into a 'no job-loss position'. How long this situation will remain is unclear. By 1985 the U.S. motor industry expects to shed 128,000 workers, or over 18 per cent of production workers, as a consequence of new heavy investment in automated equipment. This runs alongside the indirect job losses through the changes in components mentioned previously. British Leyland itself has made it quite clear through its Managing Director Michael Edwardes that the new super-mini lines at Longbridge will have to be highly automated in order to compete both in Britain and internationally.

Robots are at present hampered in their usefulness by their weight, size and relative immobility. Once programmed they can perform quite sophisticated tasks such as spraying and painting a chair or assembling a Ford motor governor with thirteen components in one-third of the time taken by an expert assembler. In Japan alone there are probably over 70,000 robots in daily use. Hitachi has developed a two-armed robot which, equipped with seven TV cameras as sensors using the Hidic 500 computer together with the 150 mini-computer, can process both visual and tactile information. This robot can assemble a spherical vacuum cleaner in $2\frac{1}{2}$ minutes. However, the development which has the greatest work impact is still being worked upon by I.B.M. This can be programmed for many different jobs and is designed for medium volume assembly work of the small variety like toasters, staplers and typewriters. In a demonstration it assembled the eight sub-sections of a typewriter in 45 seconds.

As we stated earlier, production aids such as robots will have only limited effects because of the small total of workers involved directly in the manufacturing processes of the U.K. Many of these automated concepts have been available for some considerable time but, given the high cost of the capital equipment, they have only been used for long and stable production runs. However, microprocessor control systems are making them attractive to an increasing number of employers.

The machine tool industry itself is one in which microelectronics is now being widely used in Japan and Germany. No longer are the skilled workers shown the drawings and told to knock up a machine tool. The original numerically controlled machines with their programmed paper tape 'drives' stopped this *ad hoc* method for all but the most unusual one-off tools. The new microprocessor controlled machine tools, however, have the 'software' built into the machine; programs are on floppy discs and can be changed like gramophone records. Whereas automation or computerization were often checked by software products, this will now no longer be the case. This mass production of a machine that can play many parts in the course of one day is revolutionary both in terms of the reduction of the numbers of people needed to manufacture machine tools overall and those needed to operate them.

Few manufacturing or maintenance/repair industries are immune from these changes. In tailoring there are now automatic microprocessor and laser controlled cutting and sewing machines. In footwear manufacture there are electronically controlled closing rooms. In the glass container industry there has been a 13 per cent loss of production and indirect staffs due to the installation of micro-electronically controlled equipment over the four years from 1973–6. In agriculture there are now electronic sorting machines and in California not only is research being conducted into such equipment, but agricultural research is increasingly devoted to breeding plants and animals to conform to shapes and sizes suitable for such techniques. In civil aviation there are not only computerized air traffic control, but also micro-computer aided diagnostic systems which are now also being applied to jumbo jets as well as to oil tankers. All forms of gas, liquids and radioactive sensory equipment are being manufactured with integrated circuit control.

However, it is in the non-productive areas that the main

impact on employment will occur. The 1977 Nora Report in France estimates that within ten years banks would be employing 30 per cent less staff because of technological change. Both banks and insurance companies employ large numbers of people doing 'rote' tasks which are basically repetitive. Both use large main frame computers but as yet have not really exploited the potential of disseminated data-processing. However, the cash card money dispenser machine system which not only delivers currency but also prints cheques and bank statements, is but a first and small example of the potential. From word processors to automatic debiting and clearing, inter-branch and inter-bank communications, and expansion of the credit card system up to perhaps even the cash-less society, jobs will disappear.

Insurance companies, like banks, are labour intensive. The U.K. Friends Provident company has installed visual display units in its branch offices and can display for a customer all the options of a policy and its competitor in a matter of minutes rather than days. As its Managing Director has said, this is not only more efficient, it also has cut the manpower need at head and branch offices. Again, automatic filing and the bringing forward of maturing data, the on-line computer-based information facilities available, word processing for volumes of almost standard letters and the ability to link the different branches across continents make this form of industry very vulnerable in employment terms.

The office in general is extremely under-capitalized. So many people are now working in offices and the salary bill has become so high that companies are beginning to see the advantages of automation. Moreover the grave shortage of skilled staff in the main commercial centres actually reinforces the trend. We mentioned the potential for communications and filing in an earlier chapter; now it is the turn of the word processor. It is estimated that well over a quarter of a million word processing stations are now in operation in the U.S.A. and that two or three operators can do as much work as ten typists and to a higher overall standard. In Britain the market has expanded by 10 per cent over each of the past 2 years as compared with 50 per cent in the U.S.A., but it is predicted that British growth will take off very shortly. The word processor is now looked upon as a typewriter machine with an attached screen. The typed words come on to the screen for editing, mistake correction, rephrasing, layout correction or for the insertion of information from the office databank. Obviously this makes for faster and easier letter production. The actual typing need not be done in the same office or even city: if the final form is correct, a machine in Edinburgh may type out the letter drafted in London.

This form of typing is ideal for the batch letter where either invoices, contracts, or other standard forms have to be written into personalized correspondence. Clearly at serious risk will be the more routine typing jobs. At present these machines are expensive, for an electronic typewriter, costing up to £6000, a screen processor £9000, and a 'shared resource' screen processor up to £12,000. These latter models are likely to be the machines of the future. They will have their own information banks, telecommunication links and printing facilities and, when needed, be linked into a central mini-computer information bank for extra information. Taken together with more efficient copying machines and telex facilities, collating and mailing machines, the future office will be far less labour intensive. It is also certain that the cost of these machines will fall dramatically over the next decade.

Even more alarming for those who work in offices is that the office itself may no longer be needed on the present scale. All this equipment can be installed in a manager's home or car: it will be easy to use, especially on the telecommunications side, and there may in any case be a move towards more flexible work arrangements. In turn this means fewer and smaller office blocks, leading to a reduction in the number of support and servicing staff for buildings.

Printing and journalism is another area where automation is currently making great inroads into the workforce. Many new techniques are following one upon the other. With computerized typesetting the journalist files a story and, after 'editing and subbing' it is directly set by computer, with the journalist or 'sub' making the direct input. The *New York Herald Tribune* (N.Y.H.T.) started to use this method in 1978; it now generates 200 lines an hour instead of the twenty-two of the conventional system. The total staff of the N.Y.H.T. based in Europe has been cut to only thirty as a result. Experts believe computerization of the British composing room will save 20 per cent on labour costs, whilst the form adopted by the *Herald Tribune* would save between 40 and 60 per cent of labour costs.

As a consequence of office or non-manual automation in all areas, substantial savings are being made. Football pool preparation and checking is one small instance. A small pools form which used to require 130 part-timers for roughly between 7 and 15 hours to process coupons now handles the work using two people and 3½ hours computer time. In Australia four girls working on shifts have replaced 780 men and women in one of the tax offices, merely by using a conventional computer. In holiday booking systems the tour operators are becoming more capital intensive and even in some smaller branches of government services the same is happening. Clearly everything that applies to clerical and administrative staffs in the private sector should apply equally well to the public sector. Other areas such as the money markets and the Stock Exchange, wholesaling operations, health services and mass transportation are all starting to use these new technological devices.

Design and designing teams, research and research teams will also be affected. The effects here will almost certainly have a ratchet effect on other work areas within their respective industries. By streamlining, by working for interchangeability and with microprocessor technologists, the research and design teams will inevitably be reducing the potential number of jobs available. However, as the design becomes simpler, and as the product is reduced to simple, easily made modules, so the designer is working himself or herself out of a job. Once simplification reaches a certain point the module design can be handed over to the integrated circuit manufacturers for the small amendments needed to make the small changes consequent upon the development of new chips.

There is now a growing sector of Computer Aided Design (C.A.D.). In the micro-electronics sector itself, this is already operating. It enables engineers to move more rapidly from the design stage to the layout and artwork and then directly to the driller. In mechanical engineering, engineers can now go straight from design to production without pre-engineering and without programmers because of the new screen-based design facilities which, using tape or more recently even without this aid, put the cutting paths etc, directly on to the tool.

These trends have not gone unnoticed officially. In 1977 the National Electronics Council stated that microprocessors were providing new opportunities to various industries. They named metal and plastic fabrication, instrument and electrical engineering, shipbuilding, vehicles, electronic components and assembly, office machinery and computing, aircraft, and printing and publishing. They might have added several more, for example, textile machinery and production where it is happening now, mining and bakeries. With this development it must be realized it is not the industrial sector that is the important factor, but the type of process, be it production or clerical. Once the common elements have been broken down there is no reason to isolate industries for special attention – they will automatically receive it, stemming from the changes in work patterns and the numbers of workers employed.

So far, however, we have neither studied the type of jobs most at risk, nor attempted to quantify the resultant 'collapse of work'. This is the challenge to be taken up in the next chapter. But the present summary should conclude with the following cautionary reflections: in the last 30 years the cost of computer calculations has moved in the U.S. from a few dollars for a few instructions per second to less than 1 cent for *millions* of instructions per second. The changes now have a compelling arithmetic force.

8 Where the work goes

Computers can now be programmed to test some of the brilliant chess masters, which was thought to be virtually impossible only 4 years ago. The program needed is extremely sophisticated and computer analysis of the highest ability is required as is a large, very powerful computer. It is precisely *not* this form of well published computer advance that will be at the root of the structural changes to our work environment. For the most part the systems used will be mundane, even boring standardized packages which, when put together, will fit precisely a large number of criteria and perform many jobs without a change of program or machine. This is not an attempt to 'write down' the advances; on the contrary, it is to point out that the advances will move in almost unnoticed because of their lack of colour.

The technical press in Britain dulls the most exciting advance and this, combined with its small readership, often means that technical advances are not 'picked up' by the more popular media. The seepage of ideas is slow. The computer press has at times risen above this level but is restricted by its use of heavy jargon which makes unintelligible the most interesting of subjects. It is, however, this trade and technical section of journalism that carries the stories of change or impending changes and reports them faithfully.

Most of these journals, however, have one thing in common: they have a total dependence on advertising revenues for their existence and these revenues have to come from the industry's employers. Whilst the journals describe in glowing terms technological advances, they rarely either criticize, or indeed, analyse their direct or indirect social and employment implications.

The result is a very skewed picture of the effects of the changes
and a lack of debate in an area where early discussions may well
fend-off later disasters. We have already pointed to changes that
have caused redundancies yet few employers would have admitted to them at an early stage for fear of adverse reaction. As an
editorial in *Computer Weekly* expressed it on 22 September
1977: 'But we are aware, day in and day out, of computer
systems that are being implemented which either eliminate
existing jobs or reduce the number of jobs in the future. However, few companies like to announce "our computer has saved
us *x* staff" because there is a fear of what union reaction might
be. *It is a case of a creeping death of a thousand small cuts*' (our
emphasis). We have stressed already that the changes take place
over time, are small, often apparently insignificant and disemployment is often by 'natural wastage' and undramatic. Yet
it all adds up to a considerable loss of work and even now, when
the technologies are in their infancy in Britain, jobs are being
lost.

The concept of the process as a broad advance rather than
affecting separate industries or sectors in a special way becomes
important in this chapter. It is those working with processes or
products who are at the greatest risk, not merely workers in an
industry. Few industries will disappear. Most will change. The
consequent collapse of work will thus affect certain types of
employees across the full range of industries with particular
problems in special industries arising either from accelerated or
retarded change, or immunity against change. Work will not
only collapse, it will change, and these changes will hinge
around education and thus, at least in Britain, issues of social
class.

Work in general is becoming more knowledge based. It has
become ritual for trade union leaders and politicians to
denounce 'the unacceptably high level of unemployment'
immediately after the publication of the Department of
Employment's monthly figures. This is especially so when
applied to unemployment amongst those under 20 years and in
particular to school-leavers. Yet it is a fact, acknowledged
officially but quietly, that most of the unemployed youngsters
have no qualifications whatsoever, neither C.S.E.s nor 'O'
levels. The jobs that are disappearing are the labouring,

unskilled jobs; these jobs where training for the future has always been limited and where there is nowhere to go in a promotion or work sense.

Schools have been preparing children for this type of working life for decades, but now this preparation is for the dole and perhaps despair. Of course there are qualified young people who cannot find work but much of this can be put down to accidental mismatching; the geographical accident of where people live, or the accident of skin colour. The choice of jobs is certainly wider for those with some qualifications and in the future this gap can only broaden.

'Don't put your daughter on the stage Mrs Worthington' may prove to be unsound advice in the near future, for the theatre is likely to be one of the few growth areas in employment, as leisure time becomes more available, although as any Equity member can testify there is enough unemployment there already to soak up a massive expansion. But it is not a knowledge based industry. The changes that are taking place are in petrochemicals, engineering, transport and in all areas of machinery where those who work will need new skills. Many, though obviously not all, will need technical skills of a totally new and different kind to the old crafts and craftsmen. They will be knowledge and educationally intensive skills.

The British educational system is very heavily class biased. The percentage of young people going to university or other tertiary education from social classes D or C is very low. Worse, the percentage sitting 'O' level and 'A' level examinations from these groups is also very low. Much has been written and spoken about the way the 1960s heralded the classless society, but this is really wishful thinking by those to whom social class divisions are an embarrassment. If, as we suspect, jobs in the future are going to be dependent on acquired educational skills, then unless the system changes there must develop a reinforced and stimulated class conflict. Those from the lower social class families will look forward to unemployment, the others to relatively well-paid employment. This is neither inevitable nor immutable, but it will probably be the trend, unless actions are taken to alleviate the problem.

One of the strangest phenomena in Britain today is that amidst high unemployment there are pockets of shortages of skilled labour. Skilled machinists and machine setters, doctors and dentists, radiographers and computer operators and programmers, engineers and toolmakers are all in short supply either regionally or nationally. There are a multitude of reasons for these discrepancies and they can have serious effects. For example, I.C.I. decided not to go ahead with a proposed new plant in Teesside because of a lack of skilled manpower. Incomes policies, nineteen of them since 1945, have made it uneconomical for individuals to invest *in themselves*. Their return is not only low, it has often been less than that of the unskilled person. Public sector cuts, lack of forward planning in relation to consumer demands and the semi-collapse of the apprenticeship systems have all had their parts to play in this imbalance. Economic theory suggests that these imperfections in the labour market only really begin to have effect in times of full employment and they then contribute to wage-push inflation. A strong argument can be made that as the skill requirements are changed by the new technologies, we shall be experiencing a rising level of unemployment alongside severe skill shortages and that although this should disappear within a few years it will have a considerable impact in the meantime.

What sort of jobs will be replaced? What sort of skills will be needed? The unskilled, semi-skilled and skilled manual jobs, clerical, administrative and managerial posts and the whole information industry workforce are all at risk. Clearly not all the jobs, but some of all these types of jobs are threatened. The new technologies will be capable of performing simple functions where these are predetermined; that is, all jobs which repeat one or even many operations and where personal decision making is at a minimum or non-existent, can be, though not necessarily will be, replaced by a machine. Other jobs will simply disappear because the manufacturing process has become truncated, rather like a by-pass often isolates a town or village. Others will disappear because of the indirect effects of these changes and among these could well be a different type of job where initiative has to be applied or where human reaction and judgement is paramount. In these instances it is not the machine replacing the human, it is the machine changing the process to make the skills redundant.

In the manufacturing sector there is a wide range of job titles across industries to describe the work of people in each industry. Lack of space precludes listing these titles, though it is doubtful whether it would be productive to do so. In general terms and with general descriptions the same analysis can be made, without recourse to the separate titles and without a loss in quality. Labourers or unskilled workers whose jobs are involved in the moving of parts or materials, or of bits of plant, will have restricted opportunities, as will other unskilled workers in the indirect jobs of cleaning or stacking as the processes change. The semi-skilled and skilled workers will have *even more* limited opportunities. As the logic controlled machine tools take over so the skilled man becomes a machine minder or technician; this process is either deskilling or involves the changing of skills, but in either event far fewer men will be needed. In mass production it is the semi-skilled and unskilled on the tracks, lines or stations whose jobs are at risk. Again, unskilled work in packing, sorting, grading and despatching departments will be diminished. Welders, painters, joiners, assemblers, metal shapers, furnacemen, solderers, lathe and press operators will all have, amongst others, diminishing chances of finding employment.

In the clerical area, typists, filing clerks, general office staff and switchboard operators will all find jobs harder to find. Personal or executive secretaries will probably be shielded from the changes because their skills tend to be far more in the personal judgement area and besides, managers need humans rather than machine contact to advise them and to pass on instructions. There is a great shortage of this type of staff at present which means that their future is more assured.

A major section of the work-force is employed in the area of administration, the so-called bureaucrats of our time. This recent expansion in jobs has been stimulated both by the growth in the size of enterprises and the consequent need to co-ordinate and service them, but also by the rise in public sector employment where such work is central in government practice. The new communication technologies could make large numbers of such people redundant. The administrator and his or her staff generally have the function of ensuring that others are working within the parameters laid down by the organization itself and modern equipment is being produced that enables self monitoring to be effected. At the same time forms that have to be filled in by an unsophisticated public will be simplified and reduced in numbers and so those needed to file, reject or process them will be reduced.

As the number of components, processes and employees decreases so does the need for managers, as for foremen and supervisors. Managerial jobs will disappear not only for these reasons but also because many of the jobs are repetitive, routine and involve little personal discretion or leeway. In recent years the mushrooming of managerial positions has rivalled that of administrative staffs but the technology of information, monitoring and communication will take over a substantial part of their function. Foremen and supervisors are only required where there is in operation a process involving other workers; remove that process and their jobs are removed too. As recently as ten years ago managerial staffs were felt to be immune from redundancy. Since then there have been some job losses due to mergers, collapses of enterprises and generally depressed economic conditions. However, for the first time these staffs will be in the front line of disemployment, not for a short time, but, because the jobs are actually disappearing, for ever. This phenomenon clearly also affects the prospects of potential managers.

We drew attention to design, drawing office and computer operational staffs in the previous chapter. Equally replaceable are supermarket employees at cash desks, truck drivers, wholesale trade employees, printers of all descriptions and skills, fork-lift truck drivers, and many specific skills ranging from paramedical to crafts such as panel beating. On the other hand the future for service and maintenance staff presents a different face. In the medium term there should be an explosion in the need for servicing staff. The new equipment will often need routine, pre-emptive servicing as well as stand-by staff for emergency repairs: the more capital intensive an operation, the more important these staff become. However, as machines are built with self diagnostic systems and as they become less complex and more reliable this demand will slacken off and the total number will diminish, as in other professions, over the longer term.

The job changes leading to either the de-skilling of jobs or the need for quite radical retraining may well precipitate the voluntary early retirement of many older skilled employees. Fear of the unknown or stress and boredom will take their inevitable toll. This could mean that more jobs will be created among the younger age groups and school-leavers and thereby, to some extent, relieve the pressure on that section of society.

Although the jobs are at risk, not all of them will be lost. Machines need people to operate them and to create other secondary jobs in their operation and in their production. What will happen is that there will be a reduction in these types of jobs available at the time when, over the next fifteen years, there will be an expanding potential labour force. Reductions will be in the types of jobs traditionally allocated to women – the office job, the shop job, the bank clerk – and this at a time when women represent the greatest growth in the potential labour force. Across industry and commerce, services and government, machines or systems will partially replace the types of jobs described above, or else these will simply disappear. Even the jobs that remain will change, for example the operation of a word processor requires different skills to those used by a traditional typist and a great deal of retraining will consequently be needed.

Other jobs will alter, although there is no reason to suppose that there will be a reduced demand for them. Medical practitioners (both doctors and ancillaries) will have better diagnostic and treatment aids and the technicalities of the work will change radically and rapidly. Many managerial and most professional jobs will change as the machines enable responses to be made faster; certainly in architecture, for example, there may have to be a radical rethinking in the types of industrial and commercial buildings currently being designed. Jobs in service industries such as travel agencies, booking agencies, even large hairdressers and service departments will all be able to use the new technologies for the planning of their services and this will require the grafting of new skills on to the traditional ones.

The whole area of jobs at risk can be divided into 'information workers' and others. In the former category we have already covered the secretarial and office staffs but it does of course include teaching at all levels – writing, journalism, media work, librarians, research, and telecommunications. In the U.S.A. (1975) it was estimated that half of all employees were 'information workers'. If the concept of the information revolution is correct, and there is a considerable body of research and evidence to suggest that it is, then many of these workers will be at risk from the newly accessible data-bases and telecommunication systems. Whilst many of the jobs in research and teaching require individual judgements, and personal contact, many more do not. Yet it is precisely this sort of employment that has taken up the slack caused by the diminution of employment in the manufacturing sectors.

Between 1973 and 1977 the number of employees in the service sector rose in Belgium, Holland, West Germany, U.S.A., U.K., Japan, Italy and France – by 3·2 per cent in Italy, 3 per cent in the U.S.A., down to 0·5 per cent in West Germany. Over the same period employment in industrial production fell in all of those countries. In some the Gross Domestic Product rose, in others it fell. In some industrial output rose, in others, like Britain, it fell. But the key point is that all these highly industrialized countries have been switching employment to the service sectors. Clearly this particular policy change coincides in time with a general depression in world trade which provides part of the reason for this shift. Another reason, however, is the emergence of the production capabilities of some of the less developed countries which many transnational companies are using to lower their labour costs to develop a corporate advantage.

Until now public sector employees have not been discussed although many will have been encompassed by the previous analysis. Nationalized industries tend to work on the same patterns as other industries and will be subject to the same constraints and the same advantages as private sector enterprises. They have to make profits, finance their investment and, in an increasing number of industries, compete successfully on the open market. They thus have the same incentive to apply new techniques, with the same implications as any other sectors.

Local and central government, the Health Service, education and quasi-government bodies, such as ACAS or the Housing Corporation, on the other hand, face no such constraints. They produce no measurable end product and no definable service against which an improvement or worsening of the situation can be measured. Of course it is possible to point to the frequency with which the refuse is collected, or the number of dwellings built, but these are exceptions to the local government rule. In central government it is possible to check on the ability of the 'Job Shops' to provide openings for employment or the number of miles of new motorway built, but how does one measure the success or effect of the Home or Foreign Offices, the Ministry of Defence or the Department of Overseas Development? Even in the Health Service there is a problem. Hospital waiting lists are long and this is certainly a sign of a malfunction in the system and too few resources, but it may well be that many on the lists would be better off anyway being treated in the primary medical areas.

A further complication is that apart from when there is a clear improvement in services, following the appointment of further staff in jobs which deal directly with the public (for example medical staffs, dustmen, social workers), no such scale of comparison can be applied to the majority of staff. If people are added to, or removed from the Treasury, the Finance Department of a Local Authority or the Equal Opportunities Commission, would it help or hinder the service? If government employment is intended to provide a public service, pleasant or necessary (like VAT or PAYE), it should do so in the most effective way, with the minimum of cost, and the new technologies could exert a remarkable influence towards achieving the goals especially in the information/communication areas. However, even when outside consultants are brought in to design efficient systems, things go awry. For example, McKinsey's designed the three-tier National Health Service administrative structure which by unanimous consent is now deemed to be slow, costly and inefficient in operation. Strangely enough the Minister who introduced it was the arch apostle of government expenditure cuts, Sir Keith Joseph – he didn't do so for Machiavellian reasons.

Two other factors separate this aspect of public sector employment from all other forms of employment systems. The first is that overall it is the most heavily unionized, not only in Britain, but almost over the entire world. This puts an immediate and understandable constraint on peremptory employer actions. The second is the more fundamental. In the private sector (or nationalized industries) the senior managers have certain targets. They will optimize profits, sales or market shares and in doing so will enhance their own position and perhaps ensure their own promotion. Their success is measured in external objective factors. In government there is no such measurement and success seems often to be measured by the number of people directly responsible to the senior official. So instead of aiming to maximize profit or service a government official will be tempted to 'people maximize'. When a new technology comes along which can reduce this number of sub-ordinates it may well be resisted (covertly) on the grounds that it will reduce the status of the senior official. This reinforces the position of the Civil Service and Local Government unions in that when they object to potential redundancies they are push-ing against a swinging door. What is likely to happen in this sector, therefore, is that the new technologies will be implemented, but that the present level of staffing will remain, and, what is more, will remain relatively unchanged in broad functional terms. In this respect the largest employers in Britain and overseas will almost certainly stand outside the overall work trend. What is unhealthy in this situation is not the retention of employees, but their non-transference to more productive public sector areas. There can be little doubt that public needs, especially in health, education and social services, are not being adequately met because of low staffing levels in the types of jobs which impinge directly on to the public – retrain-ing and redeployment could solve these problems.

At least two studies have been produced on the impact of technology on jobs, which have attempted to put a figure on the resultant unemployment. A French report, commissioned by President Giscard D'Estaing, was written by a senior adviser to the French Finance Ministry, Simon Nora, and although en-titled 'L'information de la Société' is known as the 'Nora Report'. Interestingly, Nora appreciated the reactions of the Civil Service, identified them in the manner we have adopted, but still thought that certain Ministers would lose up to 30 per cent of their staff. Nora did not quantify his hypothesis overall but did show that the French seventh national plan's job creation targets of 1·55 million new jobs was not even a starter. The report is interesting, not only because a high-ranking government official has reinforced the prejudice of the authors of this book, but also because of the imaginative longer term approach that it takes; an approach rarely considered useful by governments. It looks at the possibility of the internationally competitive companies dying because they have been technologically outflanked by smaller and more enterprising nationally based competitors, and it recommends the setting up of a silicon chip manufacturing capacity in France. Nora sees the coming together of companies, telecommunications, satellites and broadcasting as the most important factor in this new international industrial order and in this he is backing up the U.S./U.K. predictions of an information revolution.

We cannot agree with all of the report. For example, unless national governments decree otherwise we believe that the large transnational corporations will take over the smaller nationally based companies rather than the reverse. Whilst not giving a specific overall figure for possible unemployment in the absence of positive government (or political) counter-action, from the report's specific figures and general arguments, Nora is clearly envisaging unemployment in the range of 12–14 per cent in 20 years time. This can easily be deduced from the specific figures and general arguments made in the course of the report.

The second set of figures is contained in a lengthy report made by S.P.R.U. at the University of Sussex. This looked at the U.S. economy in terms of broad occupational groupings rather than industrial sectors: information handlers, industrial workers, service industry workers and agricultural workers. The report then graded these into high, medium, low and zero risk with respect to job loss over the next 15 years. Basing their prognosis on this, the analysts found a potential job loss of 18·2 per cent. By halving these risk factors they reduced the possible loss to 7·2 per cent, but clearly believed that the higher figure was the more accurate.

When this calculation was repeated for the U.K. the higher risk factors gave a possible job loss of 16 per cent, or roughly 4,000,000. Of course, these figures for unemployment would be in addition to the present level and should be seen in conjunction with, but not in addition to, the Cambridge and Sussex long-term arguments already outlined in Chapter 6.

The job titles which the S.P.R.U. report feels are at maximum risk are as follows: proof readers, library assistants, postmen, telegraph operators, draughtsmen, programmers, accountants and book-keepers, financial administrators, secretaries, billing clerks, key punchers, cashiers, filing clerks, meter readers, shipping clerks, TV repairmen, plateprinters, telephone repairmen, light electricians, machinists, mechanics, inspectors, assemblers, operatives, material handlers, warehousemen, sales clerks and stock clerks. Despite the American terminology, this list clearly is a matter for subjective judgement: for example, for secretaries, read typists, especially shorthand typists, and we have already argued the case for TV repairmen being relatively unaffected. Despite small differences in judgement about inclusions and exclusions from this list, it represents a sobering and thought-provoking exercise and one which it is difficult to fault in principle or indeed in identification of the magnitude of the problem.

One point must now be clarified. The long-term analyses mentioned in Chapter 6 were based on the premise of little or no growth and thus, because of the models used (or implicit), little or no technical change. In other words the competitive position of Britain remains unchanged except that it continues on its downward trend. The Nora and S.P.R.U. arguments are based on the antithesis of this. They argue that France, the U.S. and Britain respectively must change technologically and as we have argued this must work to Britain's advantage because, even if all countries use the same new technologies, Britain has in one fell swoop, caught up with our competitors and reversed the trend. There is thus a choice.

Remain as we are, reject the new technologies and we face unemployment of up to 5·5 million by the end of the century. Embrace the new technologies, accept the challenge and we end up with unemployment of about 5 million. Whilst there is a world of difference between the two consequences and the possibilities that can be exploited inherent in these strategies, the latter is by far the most favourable. What is clear is that whichever road we take work will collapse.

It is vital that some quantifications are made to assess the scale of the probable unemployment and we shall start by using a job content analysis. The 1977 New Earnings Survey stated that 47 per cent of all employment was now in the non-manual or 'white collar' category. By removing a substantial number of these, but also adding some workers from particular manual worker categories, we estimate that roughly 42–44 per cent of U.K. employees are in the 'information sector' – a sector at high risk for future unemployment. This, however, is too general a classification and we therefore need to fine down the analysis to more specific occupational groupings. These groupings do, of course, transcend the industrial sectors and are based on the 1977 New Earnings Survey data.

Certain groups will be hardly affected, if at all. Farm labourers, trawlermen, general labourers, top management and leisure employees (indeed, these may expand in number) including sports employees. Together, these account for 4·4 per cent of the labour force.

Next we consider the groups that only will be minimally affected. These include the security and protection specialists, professional staffs, catering, hairdressing and other personal services, and education, welfare and health workers. Whilst there may be some specific jobs at risk, for example, in middle management, there is a strong likelihood that, if the correct policies are adopted, these groups could actually expand. At present they account for 28·4 per cent of employment. Construction and mining at 3·6 per cent of the working population is another grouping which will be relatively proofed against disemployment.

Transport, material handling and storing and related jobs account for 8·4 per cent. These are somewhat more at risk overall but especially so in the handling and storage job areas. However, the largest single occupational grouping in the U.K. is the clerical and related, accounting for nearly 19 per cent of all workers, or, around 4½ million in 1978. The Siemens' report, which has been referred to earlier, suggested that in Germany 40 per cent of this category of worker would be redundant by the mid-1980s.

The second largest grouping is concerned with processing, making, repairing and related work and this accounts for some 14·4 per cent or 3½ million employees in 1978. Most of these occupations are in the iron, steel and metalworking industries, vehicles and shipbuilding and cover first line supervisory jobs. These are high-risk jobs in high risk areas with an average job displacement effect, we would suggest, of around 10 per cent. Other high risk classifications are making and repairing – 5·2 per cent of workers mainly in the glass, ceramics, printing, clothing, footwear, plastics, etc. industries and managers at 5 per cent of the working population, which includes production and works managers, foremen and office managers and materials processing workers – 3·2 per cent of employees based in the textile, food, drink, tobacco, paper and board industries.

Together, these high-risk occupational areas account for 55 per cent of the existing working population. Given the almost certain available labour supply in the future and certain wide assumptions, we can make an estimate of probable unemployment levels. Let us assume that by 1990 there will be a labour force of around 26 million and that the information sector of the economy has risen to 50 per cent. If we assume (less than the Siemens' Report) a 30 per cent displacement in the information sector and a far more modest 10 per cent displacement effect in the non-information sector, then by 1990 there will be 5·2 million or 20 per cent. But this is too crude a treatment and needs refining.

In what follows we present our own figures based on a paper submitted to the Trades Union Congress by the Association of Scientific Technical and Managerial Staffs (A.S.T.M.S.) Research Department. This breakdown used the job function approach, which we have just outlined, transferred into industrial sectors. It assumed that any changes in work arrangements, or shortening of overall hours or reduction in overtime will have little or no impact on the number of jobs available. Whilst this is almost certainly untrue in some industries, the demand for a 35-hour week would clearly have little extra work impact in the face of a series of technological changes of the probable magnitude we have been discussing. It is equally unlikely that overtime will be cut on a voluntary basis until basic rates are increased dramatically (say by 50 per cent in some industries), and that government action to deter overtime could only be undertaken in this new high wage environment.

The other assumption is that by and large there will be a

period of maximum adoption of the new technologies over the next 15 to 20 years. We have also attempted to quantify compensating employment factors as far as this is practicable. Clearly, new jobs will be created especially in the service sector. There will be spare resources and extra cash available through increased profits and productivity-based incomes and these will have a multiplier effect on the economy in general. Obviously there are areas of unsatisfied demand which may raise production levels and these factors have been taken into account. On the other hand we have not postulated any major change in government policy in respect of providing jobs through increasing the level of services provided since this implies a thoroughgoing change in political attitudes, and we observe no signs of this.

Given this and given the uncertainties inherent in trying to forecast anything over such a lengthy time period the estimates should be treated only as guidelines. Whilst reasonably confident that we have the direction of changes correct, the numbers are more of a guide than a prediction. In the data, short term is defined as up to 5 years; medium term as up to 15 years, and long term up to 25 years, taking us into the first decade of the twenty-first century. The sample used comprises a work force of just under 20 million but does not include the armed forces, the self-employed, or British citizens working abroad. The figures for employment in the industry are based on March 1978 data and the data is in thousands:

AGRICULTURE, FORESTRY AND FISHING

Present	Short	Medium	Long
357·3	340	300	300

Whilst some capital intensification is possible in fishing, it is unlikely that agriculture will shed much more labour. Agriculture is an industry which, if certain policy prescriptions are followed, could *expand* its workforce though we think this unlikely.

MINING AND QUARRYING

Present	Short	Medium	Long
341·7	310	280	250

Despite North Sea oil and natural gas it would seem likely that coal will be kept in production as a fall back position, notwithstanding alternative energy sources, including nuclear energy.

FOOD, DRINK AND TOBACCO

Present	Short	Medium	Long
688·7	630	500	450

Much of the industry already has a degree of automation. However, the repetitive batch processing, packaging and storage sides are over-ripe for technological innovation.

COAL AND PETROLEUM PRODUCTS

Present	Short	Medium	Long
36·9	35	30	25

Research into coal derivatives, especially petroleum, may possibly reach a commercial point but even with a large possible demand for new plastics this is a deepening capital intensive industry and likely to become more so.

CHEMICAL AND ALLIED

Present	Short	Medium	Long
428·6	430	390	360

This is a very highly competitive area with signs of over production. It is dominated by transnational corporations and the signs are that, even if the industrial processes themselves do not shed jobs, the clerical, managerial and information sides will, as well as in packaging and distribution.

METAL MANUFACTURE

Present	Short	Medium	Long
469·7	450	350	250

Japan has already moved on to virtually 100 per cent automated batch steel, pipe and tube production and Britain will have to follow or drop out of this market altogether. Most other production processes could be truncated through micro-chip technology and the attendant indirect job losses follow.

MECHANICAL ENGINEERING

Present	Short	Medium	Long
928·1	920	800	620

The development of the integrated micro-circuit controlled machine tool plus the reduction in the number of components needed to be engineered will cause reductions in both the direct and indirect labour force. But in the short term, before the introduction of these technologies, there will still be a shortage of skilled personnel.

INSTRUMENT ENGINEERING

Present	Short	Medium	Long
148·3	130	100	80

Despite the increased demand for new instruments, the new techniques of design and production will reduce the workforce. This is an industry which, if it does not adopt the new technologies, will disappear entirely. It already has to contend with a very high degree of import penetration.

ELECTRICAL ENGINEERING

Present	Short	Medium	Long
741·4	700	520	410

This industry has been suffering from a high degree of overseas competition (especially Far Eastern). It is ideally placed to know about, and take advantage of, the new techniques.

SHIPBUILDING AND MARINE

Present	Short	Medium	Long
174·7	170	120	80

Only new technical innovations or radical design changes will aid this industry against the Japanese, North Korean and emerging Latin American competition in a world glutted with ships.

VEHICLES

Present	Short	Medium	Long
786·6	750	500	400

This is a slow growth industry. There is certain to be an increased advantage in well-designed specialist vehicles. In any event the new technologies will cut the needed labour force. One unknown factor is the development of production capacities in less-developed countries (L.D.C.s) and the long-range forecast may prove to be wildly optimistic.

METAL GOODS

Present	Short	Medium	Long
535·5	540	500	430

Since much of the continuous and batch production can be microprocessor controlled so, as with all the other industries, the indirect staff are most at risk. It is, however, an industry where small units can make specialist products and this could well maintain employment.

TEXTILES

Present	Short	Medium	Long
468·3	430	300	120

This industry suffers from a combination of L.D.C. pressure and technological change both of which have drastically reduced the labour force. There is also an over-capacity for artificial fibres and competition is fierce. Although specialist textile manufactures may survive, as will the larger more capital intensive mills and plants, the prospects for future employment are extremely limited in the U.K.

LEATHER AND FUR

Present	Short	Medium	Long
40·4	40	38	35

This is a small industry often dealing in singular products. It is unlikely that production changes will lose much labour; the packaging, storage and clerical sides will.

CLOTHING AND FOOTWEAR

Present	Short	Medium	Long
365·3	350	260	220

Both clothing and footwear are under intense foreign competition. The firms in the industry are small and very labour intensive. On the cheap range side it is likely that larger units, using the new technologies for design, fitting and assembly, will be introduced. There will be a large demand for specialist top-of-the-market products.

BRICKS, POTTERY, GLASS AND CEMENT

Present	Short	Medium	Long
261·3	260	240	190

Few dramatic changes are expected in this sector. Although there might be some materials substitution, British householders and industrial building purchases are conservative in their tastes but small offices and factories handled in the new technologies will not help.

TIMBER AND FURNITURE

Present	Short	Medium	Long
258·7	255	250	220

This industry has been in slow decline over many years. Whilst new furniture shaping methods will be introduced it is expected that there will be a growth in reproduction and other specialist goods.

PAPER, PRINTING AND PUBLISHING

Present	Short	Medium	Long
536·2	500	350	250

This entire industry is likely to be a prime victim of the information revolution. Apart from newer alternate sources of information and its transmission, there is a vast list of technical changes waiting to be implemented. Despite opposition to this in the short term the pressure of the new competition will ultimately ensure that these changes are realized.

OTHER MANUFACTURING

Present	Short	Medium	Long
325·5	310	300	400

This is one area which we see expanding as small groups, often co-operatives, move into the more esoteric or less-competitive market areas. There may well be official encouragement for this to happen.

CONSTRUCTION

Present	Short	Medium	Long
1215·5	1200	1000	1000

This is a very labour intensive industry. The new technologies will affect design and planning and some skills and crafts may decrease in importance. Overall, however, we expect manpower demand to hold up well and even improve in the medium term as both industrial and house building are undertaken.

GAS, ELECTRICITY AND WATER

Present	Short	Medium	Long
339·1	340	350	350

This is another area within which we expect jobs to increase, but we are assuming that any new energy source industry employment or resource employment will be put into this category. Politically it is probable that decisions to keep the industry labour intensive will prevail. However, jobs such as meter-readers and clerical and administrative posts will be phased out.

TRANSPORT AND COMMUNICATIONS

Present	Short	Medium	Long
1413·8	1300	1000	1000

Telecommunications activity will lose service and installation jobs in the short and medium term but this will be offset partly by the greater number of installations and new techniques. The control and planning systems in transport will lose jobs but, as with the smaller products, we expect new forms of transport in the long term. There is a possibility, if the political action is taken, that this industry eventually could employ more people on both the transport and communication side.

DISTRIBUTIVE TRADES

Present	Short	Medium	Long
2657·1	2550	2000	1600

This is an enormous area where in both wholesale and retail outlets there is huge scope for microprocessor application. The drift to supermarkets and cost-conscious shoppers make this inevitable in the long term.

INSURANCE, BANKING AND FINANCE

Present	Short	Medium	Long
1136·6	1050	780	650

As the Nora Report explicitly states, these industries are labour intensive at a time when the technology exists or is about to exist to make them capital intensive. The development of automatic banking and insurance, the increasing concentration of other financial markets and the use of satellite communications will decimate the labour force in these industries over the longer term.

PROFESSIONAL AND SCIENTIFIC

Present	Short	Medium	Long
3589·3	3650	3500	3650

We expect an increase in the long term in this sector as countries invest heavily in research to achieve competitive trade advantages. We also expect demand to increase (and to be met) for professional, personal and other services.

PUBLIC ADMINISTRATION

Present	Short	Medium	Long
1872·1	1600	1700	1800

As we explained earlier we expect that the public administration sector will not only hold its own in employment terms, despite the introduction of new technologies, but actually to increase. Growth is likely in the number and the scope of government agencies and this will be duplicated in government policies around the world.

MISCELLANEOUS SERVICES

Present	Short	Medium	Long
2249	2100	2100	2000

This section covers a variety of industries, both large and small, many of which are in the entertainment, leisure sector. Whilst we would see cinema, garage and vehicle servicing staff all diminish, we would also see the leisure activities employment expanding. Equally, the growth in the numbers of unemployed in the other sectors should mean a rise in the amount of do-it-yourself undertaken and reduce employment in some service industries.

We started in March 1978 with a sample labour force of 22,365,700. By the end of 1983 we expect this to be down to 21,340,000 – a reduction of just over 1 million jobs or 4·6 per cent of the total. By the end of 1993 we expect this to have fallen to approximately 18,560,000 – a reduction of nearly 3,800,000 or 17 per cent, and by the year 2003 we expect this labour requirement to have fallen to 17,140,000 – a reduction of roughly 5,200,000 jobs or 23·2 per cent. The slow start to this trend is, we believe, mainly due to the conservative attitude of British managements and reflects the Department of Industry's surveys on intentions to use technological advances, whilst the slowing down of the growth of disemployment reflects the longer term economic multiplied effects starting to work.

Most of these projections can be argued with, for they are hardly precise. Nevertheless they do point and quite independently, in roughly the same direction as regards employment as the Nora or S.P.R.U. reports. Reiterating our earlier point, the future has either to be this form of job loss or the Cambridge-school type of unemployment – the two are at opposite poles of the investment and productivity dilemma and in a very real way are mutually exclusive alternatives. The implications of the evidence advanced in this chapter are clear enough. We need to plan for this new technologically based society and we need to cope with the unemployment that will result. Both of these simple premises conceal a minefield of unexploded myths, power struggles and political steps which we shall explore in a later chapter.

9 *The international dimension*

Britain can now be conceptualized as a small microprocessor in a very large world computer, and one which controls the peripheral rather than the central parts. The importance of international trade to Britain far outweighs the importance of Britain to international trade. But there is no reason to mourn for the lost empire and none to mourn for the consequent loss of economic and political status.

We have looked at the role of international trade as it affects employment and the British balance of payments and economic policy. This, however, is not the sum total of the international dimension which in fact divides itself into two main sections i.e. the experiences and problems of those countries overseas and the internationalization of trade, technology and unemployment and the various international responses to them.

Britain is not (and will not be) the only country experiencing high unemployment. The rate at which the British are likely to take up the new technologies compared with most of their competitors does, in fact, argue that other countries will have technological structural unemployment well before we do and may be seeking to alleviate the resulting problems in their own ways. From a British point of view, this has the disadvantage of making us even less competitive in the short term with the inevitable consequences of falling exports, rising imports, deflation domestically and increasing short-term unemployment. But it also has the advantage of giving us a little time to learn from others' mistakes both in respect of the new processes and the resultant social upheavals. Providing this time is used productively and we learn to plan for the future, then if the technological implementation is not too long delayed (3 or 4 years is the most we can survive) the balance of advantages may well be ours.

From public statements and from actions of governments the notion of technological unemployment is clearly not one confined to Britain. Trade unionists, researchers and politicians are realizing the potential for good and evil and are opening up discussions. In Belgium they have gone further and the unions have started to reduce the working week. The demand of the General Labour Federation of Belgium (F.G.T.B.) is for a 36-hour week for all by the end of 1980. Despite considerable opposition from employers, department store staff have now signed an agreement which will lead to this and public sector employees (25 per cent of the whole workforce) have secured a commitment for a 38-hour week in 1979. In themselves these developments are far less important than the reasoning behind them.

Belgium is suffering from economic recession, has high unemployment and, like Britain and most other industrialized countries, will have a steadily increasing number of people in the workforce until the mid-1980s. The Belgian unions, however, are worried about technological unemployment. As George Debune, the General Secretary of the F.G.T.B., wrote in July 1978, 'Whether in printing, metal based manufacturing, banking and insurance or the distributive trades, progress on productivity, particularly when related to the introduction of electronics and data processing, seems to pose a threat to employment in these sectors. As regards employment, therefore, we cannot see any light on the horizon.' The unions supported a pre-pension scheme, similar to the British 'job swap' scheme, and though it would seem to be more successful, it was soon realized to be inadequate, in the face of the intractable and longer term difficulties.

At which point the unions decided that they would make the 36-hour week the priority bargaining point, even though at the expense of increased earnings. As George Debunne states: 'it is a balance freely arrived at, without any form of incomes policy'. According to Belgian calculations a 10 per cent reduction in working hours (the demand itself) will reduce potential unemployment by 5 per cent and, in Belgian terms, will thereby save or create 100,000 jobs; which is less than one-third of those currently unemployed. The scheme certainly represents a bold action by the unions, but, by their own admission, one which will not get anywhere near solving the unemployment crisis. It is, however, a praiseworthy action in its own right and certainly a useful example to trade unions in other countries.

West Germany has also been contemplating larger scale unemployment in the future and, although its indigenous population has been sheltered by pre-emptive dismissals and then the repatriation of 'guest workers', domestic unemployment stands at over 1 million. In a country unused to industrial action, 1978 saw both the metal workers and the printing unions go on strike over the introduction of new technical processes based on the microprocessor. The strike of the print workers involving highly skilled staff was particularly bitter. The Federal German Employers' Association took collective responsibility for the printing and publishing employers and a strike of over 2,000 was turned into a lock-out of 45,000. An agreement was finally signed in April 1978 setting out printers' duties and rights and constraining those of publishers and journalists. Despite the partial success of the dispute the new technology is now in operation, and there has to be progressively fewer jobs for skilled printers, especially as the agreement only lasts for 8 years.

Belgium and West Germany are not the only countries to have acknowledged the menacing problem of developing technology and growing unemployment. The Canadian Government has commissioned reports on new technologies; the South Korean Government has produced plans for the future based on micro-electronic technologies. The Scandinavian unions are concerned, and the Swedish Government has had to change its philosophy from retraining everyone for new jobs to substituting adult educational programmes.

It is not, then, just Britain that is worried or is starting to feel the impact. But Britain is almost alone in doing nothing central about it, and in having leading politicians who can ignore it. There are, however, the other international dimensions and these are most important as they ultimately will govern the relations between the different countries in the world. Countries, developed or less developed, capitalist or communist, are linked by international trade. They are also linked by trans-national companies which now operate in almost all countries. These vast corporations often dictate the patterns of trade and in less-developed countries (L.D.C.s) the pattern of development. They have the ability to switch finance anywhere in the world at a moment's notice and the capability of exploiting the resources of a country, effectively at will. Because they are trans-national and their responsibilities and operations are global, they are interested in the concept of global profits. This is important to realize, since in a global strategy a corporation may be satisfied to make a loss in some countries if this loss can be turned into a greater overall profit through transfer pricing and manipulation of differing tax regimes. Some companies have operated in Britain and reported a loss almost every year, but as soon as the effective rate of tax dropped to almost zero in 1976 their profits suddenly and dramatically recovered.

The German press has been full of articles on microprocessors, 'job killers' as they are labelled. At the same time firms have closed down in the clock-making, sewing-machine and cash register industries as well as teleprinters. Some estimates project unemployment of over 2 million by 1985 and certainly the firm of Siemens have suggested that, by 1990, 40 per cent of office jobs will have disappeared – which accounts for 2 million jobs. Ulrich Briefs of the Economic and Social Research Institute believes that 'all occupational categories' will be affected by the forthcoming collapse of jobs, and adds 40 per cent unemployment in the metal-working industries.

There is also a growing militant environmentalist lobby in Germany which, as in France, is having some success at the polls. Its members believe in direct action and their ranks have been swelled by those who see the present technological advances as a threat to jobs, as well as to life styles or public health and safety. Recently the unions have joined forces with this movement and successfully stopped the demonstration of a new high speed train system.

In the U.S.A. there has been an active movement to reduce working hours and these are now down to 38·2 hours per week on average, though this excludes agricultural and white-collar workers. The *United States Labor Bulletin* No. 3, 1978 notes the connection between hours worked and unemployment with wry humour. It calculates that if the colonial laws of the

Massachusetts Bay Colony for building tradesmen were still in existence (and in 1860 they were still very similar) then the 70–75 hour week, combined with no vacations or early retirement would mean that the current output of the U.S.A. could be met by half the labour force – or even less. The A.F.L. – C.I.O. has made the shorter working week a clarion call and agrees that 'the strongest push comes from a desire to protect and increase jobs'.

Governments, unions and employers have realized that basic computerization creates problems and have also realized, early in the day, that semi-conductor technology will dwarf these. The Norwegian unions have data-processing stewards and data-processing agreements. The stewards discuss, in advance of technical change, the implications to *all* employees of its introduction and the agreement delineates how and when it will be introduced. In Sweden new studies have shown that the computer, far from creating jobs as had first been thought, has actually lost them in net terms. The calculations show that from 1965 to 1975 30,000 new jobs were created whilst 90,000 were lost.

Ireland has somewhat different problems in that the state is still in the process of industrialization. However, a 1978 Green Paper on unemployment is committed to reducing it to zero by 1983. In this process the 'tax holiday' system, at present used quite extensively, will be widened – this gives employers, especially trans-national corporations, special tax advantages and other grants if they set up shop in Ireland.

Worker co-operatives, especially with work-sharing, will be explored as will budgetary welfare services expansions. It remains to be seen whether, in the light of technological advances, this programme will be successful in its objectives; the authors believe that if implemented it may provide for improved unemployment pay but little else, especially as the underlying economic conditions are shaky.

Australia is suffering from massive unemployment and although some of this can be attributed to the world recession and part to Britain's entry into the E.E.C., which changed Australia's traditional market patterns, much of it can be ascribed to their use of the latest Japanese and American capital equipment. The government had to introduce a very hard, deflationary budget in order to reduce its internal borrowing requirement, most of which is supporting the unemployed. The radical changes can be found in many industries. A plant employing twenty-four fulltime staff is making nearly all the beer cans for Australia (twelve part-timers 'do' South East Asia). The machines are self-diagnostic and contractors come in automatically if repairs are needed, and then only for 1 day. The Australian supermarkets are already implementing the U.S. system with the consequent heavy job losses, whilst the newspapers are in the first stages of revolutionary re-equipment. The telecommunications and electronic industries have shed 30 per cent of their labour force over the past 3 years and the new electronic telephone exchanges now pose a new problem. The Australian Telecommunications Employees Association (A.T.E.A.) combatted this by a novel form of industrial action. For 7 weeks they did no servicing and then refused to service or read telephone meters. The public not only were not inconvenienced, they had free calls. The result was a no-redundancy agreement with the employers.

Trans-national companies have, until now, been the leaders in industrial technological development for the basic reason that they have had both the finance and resources to devote to research and development. It is 'up to now' because the latest wave of technological change has been stimulated and developed by new smaller companies. Trans-nationals are, however, adopting the new technologies and, as we have already noted, starting to absorb these smaller high technology companies. In normal circumstances a government has a more difficult task in framing national economic objectives or plans when faced by the presence of trans-nationals. Recent 1978 events in the U.K. affecting Chrysler and past events in Chile with I.T.T. show the range of problems that governments face. However, the new technologies give these companies an added leverage over government policy and make individual national action that much more difficult to take. Indeed, it may be that only concerted international pressure over a wide front can solve individual countries' problems. Any one country which takes a decision unfavourable to the trans-national stands the risk of it moving some or all of its operation to a more hospitable host nation. If all countries take the same action, such a response is not possible; if a few key nations have the same policies, this response is not possible either. Whilst a company might be prepared to lose good will, markets or both in one country, it cannot do so if the countries opposing it represent too great a slice of its operations. In short, it is a bargaining situation and one where the bluff of the companies has not yet been called, essentially because international co-operation was not forthcoming. We would argue that the probability of high structural unemployment is just the spur that is needed to deal with this missing co-operation.

The 1950s, 1960s and 1970s saw an increasing tendency for new plant to be located in the less-developed countries (L.D.C.s) or the countries of Comecon. This represented a large change in tactics. Up to this point in time, the L.D.C.s had been treated as suppliers of cheap foods, raw materials and, in some instances, pools of exported labour, and as a market for manufactured goods. The reason for the change was that technology had advanced to the point where one production process could be easily broken down and components assembled anywhere. As the processes became more fragmented, so they became extremely easy to perform. A relatively unskilled labour force could, by using easily handled, sophisticated equipment, make components or indeed whole products. In addition to this, developments in transport, containerization, pallets, jumbo jets and huge bulk carriers made transport over long distances a cheaper proposition. This spurred and stimulated the trans-nationals. The more points of production, the more transfer pricing, and the more opportunities for reducing global tax payments means that global profits can be increased.

The L.D.C.s have offered several advantages. Wages, including fringe benefits, are low, amounting to perhaps only 10–20 per cent of those paid in industrial countries. The hours worked are often very long and there is little protective legislation of any kind; no health and safety provisions, little social security and no job protection. This cost and effort advantage is maintained through an almost inexhaustible supply of labour which has been and is being displaced from the land as farming tends to become more capital intensive. A German research paper has entitled this phenomenon 'the worldwide industrial reserve army'. In Eastern Europe the attraction has been stable environment and a balanced, well-behaved, literate and numerate labour force which, additionally, had a relatively low labour cost.

The new technologies have had an impact on this situation and will continue to do so, although on what time scale no one is yet sure. For these are as available to L.D.C.s as anyone else, and South Korea, Mexico, Iran, Singapore and now Brazil are starting to take advantage of them. The South Koreans invested in their shipyards to the extent that they are now threatening to put even the Japanese out of business. They also produce sophisticated and cheap electronic calculators, hi-fi sets, cassette recorders and the Hyundi Pony car which is being produced on automated mass production tracks. President Giscard D'Estaing summed up this development as follows: 'There have always been low wages in the world. . . . What is new is that these countries can now acquire the same technologies as we can, that is, they can manufacture the same goods as we make, but with much lower wages, taxes and social charges. That means that the advantages that we have had as industrialized countries are now being neutralized by the access of these new countries to technology.'

The problem is thus two-fold: the indigenous manufacturer, often the state, taking advantage of low costs and high technology, and the trans-national company attempting to do the same. It is interesting to note that the countries which are attempting this technologically-based industrial breakthrough are, almost without exception, right-wing and repressive regimes. The new technologies, however, add a new dimension to this situation as far as the trans-nationals are concerned.

Certainly the ability to simplify and to miniaturize components is an aid to the global industrial diversification process. The new simplified assembly techniques and others, such as automatically controlled cloth-cutting machines, also help in this dispersal. The labour force needs to be less trained than ever before, and productivity can rise out of all recognition to the previously attainable levels. The only additional costs are in increased servicing capabilities. Given it is in the trans-nationals' interests to geographically diversify for the reasons outlined above and also because it safeguards production should there be trouble in any one country, it would seem that this trend will be reinforced. This, however, is by no means so clear-cut a decision for a company.

If a company becomes very capital intensive, then the cost of labour relative to other costs is historically diminished. If this continues, then the cost of labour becomes less important in the company's calculations. Technology has introduced other considerations: redundancies following a switch of production tend to give a bad public image in a company and may affect sales, or because of other commitments, the company may wish to keep on good terms with the original host government. In such a combination of circumstances the trend may well be in the opposite direction, i.e. back to the industrialized world. However, the new technological operations may prove to be very cheap compared with the old capital intensive methods and in such an eventuality there will be a reinforcing of the existing movements towards the L.D.C.s. The authors do not pretend to know which will occur in the new circumstances but it is clear that over the past 3 years there has been a shift of work back to the industrialized countries.

Whether this is due to technology and is permanent or whether it is a response to political uncertainties in the L.D.C.s, or government blandishments in the West (and North) is not yet clear: what is clear is that the situation will not remain static.

If the jobs come back to the industrial world, then the North–South dialogue will become harsher. If, on the other hand, they gravitate to the L.D.C.s, then Northern governments and trade unions will react in a hostile manner and it is probable that a restrictive rather than a constructive social clause will be added to the General Agreement on Trade and Tariffs (G.A.T.T., the guiding light of world trade). The social clause, which is being pursued with some vigour by the T.U.C. and with a degree less enthusiasm by the British Government, would make it possible for one country to refuse to import another country's goods if that country's employers were not observing minimum standards of protective legislation, social security, health, dismissal and other social matters. It was not intended to be defensive, although in present circumstances it is being argued on defensive lines. The concept is to protect workers from exploitation in other countries and to raise the standard of living and the quality of life for workers in L.D.C.s. Yet, whichever way the jobs finally go, the North–South dialogue will be impaired.

At present there are great technology gaps in the world. The industrialized countries and their trans-national corporations control the outlets of information and their use through patent and licensing systems. The L.D.C.s are, of course, on the wrong side of the gap. This is partly an educational problem and partly deliberate policy. Yet it now appears that this gap is closing and will close still further. Since, as President Giscard noted, the microprocessor technology can be applied simply and easily, it cannot be long before other countries in Africa, Asia and Latin America start to use it. It may not be beyond the realms of possibility that by the end of this century Britain and probably other major manufacturers may not be producing volume cars or TV sets or other mass production goods. Since the assembly processes are those of low technology and the new systems can make redundant many of the residual skills still involved, then an advanced L.D.C. should have no difficulty in setting-up a manufacturing capacity, and undercutting the traditional makers, including Japan which might well become the target. Whilst almost unthinkable in present-day terms, this may appear a natural move in 20 years' time. One E.E.C. study document produced in 1976 has accepted this change and suggested that the member states should concentrate on design, high technology production and systems, services, education etc, and leave low technology production and assembly to the South.

Satellites have internationalized technological advance. Telecommunications are now literally global without the need for cables and long delays on calls due to mechanical obstructions. The use of satellites with computer links which will make data bases available across continents merely by pressing buttons or dialling, is now starting and will soon expand. After TV signals satellite transmission has now started to revolutionize the newspaper industry, it will not be too long before a Wall Street Journal reporter will file his copy on voice recognition from London direct on to word processors in the U.S. from where it will be copied, edited and automatically set. The next step is to have the London correspondent do these tasks, too. The advance might not be in everyone's interests but it seems inevitable.

The insurance industry has commissioned feasibility studies on the use of satellite transmission to co-ordinate and centralize its worldwide businesses. Understandably, the unions of the Australian insurance industry were very worried about their prospects, when they found out that salesmen and clerks will be able to file their policies, claims etc, direct through to London or New York where they would be processed, checked and money authorized, or not, as the case may be. Such a change can only be at the expense of jobs in Australia. But this could have even more serious repercussions on developing countries.

The British Insurance industry is firmly entrenched across most of Africa, the U.S. industry across most of Latin America. Africa suffers in general from a lack of trained literate and numerate workers who could form the basis of a civil service and other infrastructure bodies. In this respect the jobs and training that insurance companies give are invaluable. The satellite communication system would, however, remove the need for many of these employees and thus the training would stop which would have most unfortunate social and political repercussions.

But why should the work come to the U.K.? Why not to industrious, English-speaking Hong Kong or Manila? Or, when the jump to numerology has taken place, why not anywhere? For the first time in human history clerical work can now be exported, and in bulk.

There is a thriving, almost stateless international community in the world. The United Nations and all its agencies, the O.E.C.D., I.M.F., World Bank, E.E.D. and international union secretariats float above or between countries. This community is often well intentioned, but ineffective, partly because to be effective means alienating somebody somewhere which these bodies are loth to do and partly because they have no real power bases and thus no critical leverage. The Trade Union Secretariats are no exception to this generalization. Some, like the International Metalworkers, Transport Workers or Chemical Workers Federations, are most competent and more thrusting than others, and some have created European (Brussels orientated) subsidiaries to cope with the E.E.C. Most of these bodies, however, have anticipated the problems which are likely to arise over the next 20 years and some are trying to get united action.

The European Metal Workers Federation (E.M.F.) have produced a Charter, asking for, amongst other things, a shorter working week. In their turn the Belgians have realized the value of international co-operation. As George Debunne put it, 'The certainty that this measure (the 36-hour week) would be generally adopted at European level in the near future would undoubtedly be a powerful argument in our negotiations with the employers.' The problem is that neither the E.M.F. nor any other secretariat actually negotiates with anyone nor do they have any mandatory powers over their affiliates. Inevitably this constrains their usefulness. They can, however, exercise one very useful function and that is to enable trade unionists from different countries to meet and analyse common problems. This can in turn be translated into bilateral or multilateral action against employers and in situations where production is becoming so internationally dispersed, this is a necessary defence mechanism. They can also talk to and advise trade unionists in L.D.C.s for, in the long term, it is only trade union political pressure which will force these countries into providing the basic amenities at work now envisaged in industrial countries. However limited the role they play, these organizations will still have to be encouraged by trade unions. A concerted international approach on unemployment, preferably pre-emptive in nature, is not only desirable, but essential.

The European Trades Union Confederation acts as a policy cornerstone for common action amongst the European trade unions and at present it recognizes that unemployment is the major problem and is pressing the E.E.C. Commission to issue directives on a shorter working week and the limitation of overtime. The new European Trades Union Institute, which has been formed to undertake research projects, has the new microprocessor technology high on its list of priorities. However, the fact that the E.E.C. has not acted and also that microprocessors are not the priority, shows up the limitations of both bodies in influence and in imagination.

Both the United Nations and the O.E.C.D. have produced codes and charters on the character and behaviour of trans-national companies. Both recognize the dangers in their being large enough to be 'above' nation states. Both recognize that something should be done. Both recommend that the corporations themselves voluntarily should accept the constraints proposed in these charters. Neither are in a position to enforce the propositions as they have no laws to enforce and no penalties to be inflicted. Neither document recognizes a pending unemployment problem. The O.E.C.D.'s McCracken report is even more disappointing. Whilst it recognizes that unemployment exists, it deals only with the short term and totally discounts technological unemployment. It acknowledges the danger of unemployment '. . . but there can be no complacency about the consequences of prolonged unemployment on social, racial, religious and regional tensions, and in this, on attitudes to work and society in general. Indeed, the continuation of excessively high levels of unemployment could call into question the market oriented system.' In other words, unemployment represents a great danger to capitalism. Having stated this, however, the report then ignores all but short-term unemployment problems.

The International Labour Office (I.L.O.), the trade union arm of the United Nations, is even more disappointing. It produced papers in the 1960s based on the original computer scare stories, but has not broached the subject since in a concerted fashion.

Both of the authors were and continue to be convinced that the U.K.'s entry into the Common Market was an unmitigated disaster, and we believe that to date we have been proved to be correct. On the other hand, the European Economic Community has a property which makes it unique amongst international organizations. It has laws of its own which transcend national laws, it has a court, which can impose fines, and imprison theoretically, for contempt of its courts. In the probable situation of high unemployment in which we will find ourselves, these features take on an attractive appearance where they would otherwise appear repugnant. For no one country can take full remedial action against mass long term unemployment on its own, unless it applies tariffs, boycotts and other interventions. The cost of job creation, of work sharing or even of advanced leisure activities must result in many expensive developments. If the cost of extra employment were applied directly to an employer, this would put that company at a comparative disadvantage and unless the economy was permanently closed to imports, would probably cause significant damage. If, however, the Government decides to pay for work sharing, education, training, job creation, leisure actitivies and the like, it will need to raise a vast amount of revenue. As fewer people will be working the bulk of this will have to come from corporate taxation. So given the trans-national domination of the British economy, it might pay the companies to move elsewhere, unless they wanted a tax loss. Even if they stayed, the odds would be on their 'making' minimal profits so that even high nominal rates of tax would yield very little (this would be done through transfer pricing) and the government schemes would founder for lack of money. Of course it would be possible to take most of industry and commerce into public ownership so that profits accrued directly to the state. Whilst this, the most radical option, is also the most feasible, it is true that the trans-national is now so integrated that one would be taking over a 'shell' rather than a fully fledged operation. This could be overcome, but only after a considerable time and the resulting social ferment, given the high unemployment already present, would mean that this time was not available; it would be a genuinely revolutionary situation.

The E.E.C., however, could make it mandatory upon countries to reduce the working week, to equalize corporation taxation and to develop similar job sharing schemes. When confronted with this huge market activity, and collective action, the trans-nationals could do nothing but accept or lose their markets.

It has been argued that the E.E.C. is a capitalist club which could not and would not take such action. The one certain thesis of capitalism is that it changes and adapts to given circumstances; it adapts in all its outward and physical manifestations because it wishes to survive. It will accept lower profits rather than no profits at all. The E.E.C., because it is basically capitalist, has therefore a vested interest in maintaining the fundamental *status quo*. It is also an interventionist body, not at all *laissez-faire* in its approach to business. The McCracken report gave the game away: long term unemployment could destroy the goose that lays the golden egg and the E.E.C. would certainly try to ensure that eggs were still laid, even if they had to be made of silver gilt.

Thus, if any one institution can take the effective action required, it will be the Common Market. There is no reason why, with a different political direction there should not be E.E.C. wide nationalization, although this may seem to be heading into the realms of fantasy. There is also some room for inter-country development of projects to create labour intensive industries or leisure facilities. Indeed, there are a great many positive actions the E.E.C. could undertake to encourage and develop high technology and take the initiative in improving the quality of life.

These, however, assume a concerted and very radical change in governmental policies, not only of the existing nine member states but probably also Greece, Spain and Portugal. (These three countries together could add considerably to the overseas unemployment problem.) The E.E.C. laws on mobility of labour coupled with the interchangeability of social security provisions could mean millions of migrant unemployed workers trekking around Western Europe looking for jobs. Such a situation would confirm the worst fears of the McCracken report and reinforce our own conviction that the E.E.C. might actually act.

Admittedly it is difficult enough at present to foresee a substantial change in political attitudes in Britain, let alone across the E.E.C., to make such positive strides a possibility. Though if any single country does so act it will almost certainly be Britain. A new and proper social contract domestically is possible – a European one is most unlikely. International action is, however, only one prerequisite, whether it comes through the E.E.C. or co-ordinated trade union pressures. But many options are open to cope with the situation and in the next chapter we shall survey these in relation to the problems we anticipate, before going on to describe how we see the future in Britain.

10 The broad choices

Work is inextricably entwined with income in industrialized societies and thus clearly has a value as income equals goods equals standard of living equals status. Jobs themselves impart status. At one time an office job was highly prized because it involved wearing decent clothes, less washing at the end of work and clean hands; work, although elevated by the establishment, was not to be seen to be done. Nowadays, a high status value is attached to different jobs. Doctors, nurses, architects, barristers and university professors are all ranked high in the public esteem, yet solicitors, dentists, teachers and scientists are all regarded as inferior. The more mundane jobs – the factory assembler, the packer, the check-out operator, the bus conductor and the refuse collector – tend to have little intrinsic value in themselves if displayed for public esteem, whilst the administrator is universally disliked. For the majority of people, though not some professionals, it is work, not the job that is important to them for public recognition or approbation. But is it?

Work became important in the industrial revolution, a revolution that was heavily dependent on Protestant values. People had to work, otherwise capitalism would have halted at an early stage. Some of the arguments, especially from the Church of England and non-conformist churches, so played on the emotions that they verged on George Orwell's 'double think'. So far there has not been an opportunity of testing the hypothesis that in industrial societies work is an over-rated commodity. But in some of the Opec countries, for example – and Kuwait is a prominent example, the revenues from oil are so great that most nationals do not work (imported labour does that), but they do not appear to be suffering from deprivation as a result. In the more primitive societies work is undertaken solely to obtain food, create shelter and clothes and perhaps create a surplus to trade for another person's different surplus. The rest of the time is spent at leisure activities. These societies do not appear to suffer from deprivation of work, although other deprivations are rife.

We do not believe that work *per se* is necessary to human survival or self-esteem. The fact that it appears to be so is a function of two centuries of propaganda and an educational system which maintained the 'idea' of work as its main objective, but which singularly failed to teach about leisure and how to use it. This is not to say that a lack of work, even with a reasonable amount of money attached to it, would be acceptable to society as it stands at the moment; indeed this would be patently untrue. People at present accept that they will be bored if out of work, and so become bored; they believe they will drift, and they drift; they believe that by not working they will become useless, and too many become useless. This need for work is, we would argue, an ingrained and inculcated attitude of mind. Children have learned from their parents that work is essential, and their parents from their parents, and within the family circle, let alone outside, work has taken on the attributes of a shibboleth.

It is, of course, not only capitalist societies that encourage the work ethic. The communist societies all have work as a prime objective and treat it as the most precious of commodities even to the extent of sacrificing possible increases in the standard of living to guarantee its maintenance.

But if work is not the natural state of mankind, then why have we spent so long demanding it? It is almost a conditioned reflex of the trade union movement to oppose unemployment, and though this is understandable in the conditions prevailing today, and in the past, of little money and a great deal of stigma, would it make so much sense if conditions were to alter? But for them to change there needs to be a revolution both in attitudes and in expectations. Such a change must start in the schools and be reinforced by parents and friends, but like the Sex Discrimination Act, it will take a long time to alter inbred assumptions. Yet, if conditions were to change, would not today's responses to tomorrow's crisis be anachronistic?

If a society can be shaped so as to provide goods and services to satisfy people according to at least today's standards and can do so by employing many fewer people, which would be the best approach: to spread out the available work, or to rearrange work to permit extended leisure by drawing on the latest resources? We are convinced that the second alternative would be the more acceptable and desirable.

In earlier chapters we have attempted to show that the new technologies, especially those based on the microprocessor and other micro-electronic breakthroughs, along with an expanding labour force and declining traditional industries, will precipitate and then create large scale, permanent disemployment. This view is shared, it would seem, by foreign politicians, researchers and trade unionists. Given contemporary society and the attitudes that have been evolved, what problems are likely to emerge?

In both modern industrial states and the developing nations, governments have found it expedient to foster rising expectations of material goods. This is as true of a centralized communist state as of a Western parliamentary democracy. Governments which do not stimulate the conditions for such a growth to take place are often superseded.

Citizens in all the industrialized countries have thus had continuously rising expectations of an acceptable material standard of living. To fulfil these expectations, the overwhelming majority have to work and whether this is as an unskilled production worker, a senior manager or a brain surgeon, is irrelevant. If, in these circumstances, a considerable number of people are denied these expectations because of unemployment, inevitably they will feel deprived. It would be as though overnight a caste system had been imposed with the unemployed fulfilling the role of the untouchables. It is an unfortunate commentary on society in general that unemployment only becomes an issue of concern when it reaches high levels, but for each unemployed person it is a matter of great concern from the first days. Nevertheless it is true that the problems surrounding an unemployment level in the U.K. of 500,000 or even 1,500,000 differ in both magnitude and kind from those arising from a level of 5 million or more. The sheer weight of such numbers would make them a potentially potent political and social force. To be fair, probably no one in Britain some 5 years ago would have believed that unemployment could have reached its present levels without serious trouble. That there has been so little is in no small measure due to the trade unions' belief, however misguided, in the ability of the Labour Government's policies to reduce unemployment and the consequent lack of public pressure together with workers' gut feeling that they would be protected in some way. Both authors claim immunity from any responsibility attaching to this, because they have consistently warned that the policies had no chance of achieving what was promised.

Yet there have been some significant changes in behaviour, which are no doubt fostered by high unemployment. Vandalism and crime have increased, especially crimes committed by young persons, racialism has reared its head and intolerance has perceptibly grown. All these were symptoms of unemployment in the 1930s. The present general tolerance of high unemployment, notable in other industrial countries too, has happened despite political attempts to mobilize reactions, attempts which too often proved to be counter-productive. What it does mean, however, is that the magic threshold figures have lost their validity; how often have we all heard, 'wait until unemployment reaches one million, the British will never stand for it'? They have. At the same time the concept of unemployment insurance has collapsed and one in ten of British citizens are now supported directly or indirectly by means tested monies from the Supplementary Benefits Commission. But 5 million is a different matter altogether, and even 4 or 3 or perhaps 2 millions will prove to be a trigger point for the inevitable disruption. Socially deprived, cut off from the consumer society, and from a society generating more wealth than ever before, such a large number of people is bound to be a destabilizing factor. If the conventional political system is not capable of solving their problems, then the unconventionals will say that they can. From both the far Left and far Right claims will be made that the present system is responsible for the plight of the unemployed and action will be advocated outside of the normal political channels. Such a representation is by definition unorthodox and, more to the point, often violent.

From a purely economic point of view, unemployment at

these high levels will prove very difficult to fund in the present context of taxation. It has been estimated that the 1·5 million unemployed, would, if employed, completely eliminate our £9 billion borrowing requirement. For not only would there be a huge saving in unemployment pay and other social security and supplementary benefits, but also because income tax and sales taxes would then be paid. On the other hand if 5 million were unemployed the tax system would have to be oriented very differently to finance the resulting deficits. Although some Conservative politicians might find it attractive to cut unemployment pay and other benefits that would be the most counter-productive thing to do – they would actually have to be increased substantially or, to put it another way, if national policy puts you out of work, national economic policy must pay you.

Neither side of industry will be immune from the changes. In the company sector mergers, closures and reorganizations will be prevalent, with all the attendant worries and alarms, even down to the certainty that all existing job evaluation schemes will have to be re-worked. Management will thus be under greater pressure than ever before. On the trade union side, some unions, especially those based on a single craft or skill, may well find themselves with few members as these skills are replaced by machines and technicians. Unions in the print, metalworking, tobacco and a host of smaller industries will be affected. There is now a grey-collar area to add to the existing blue- and white-collar areas and it is clear that there will be a substantial merger movement over the next decade with a reduction in the total number of unions.

Politically and socially unemployment poses deep problems with vandalism, crime and a general alienation all likely to increase. In addition a different set of difficulties will affect a different section of the population. The new technologies will not only make people workless, they will change the skills needed for a very high percentage of people who remain at work. This will require a massive expansion of in-house training. Whilst this is possible, it neglects the problem in human terms. People dislike change, and even more so when the change is forced upon them rather than them volunteering for it. Change disturbs those pre-conceived ideas and preset routines which all of us find comforting; the result may well be more than a slight degree of volatility amongst those still at work. Coupled with this is the high probability that promotion patterns will be disrupted. As new skills become important the workers trained in them will gain promotion ahead of those with the conventional skills who, in the nature of things, have had every right to expect it. Similarly, whereas the foremen and supervisory grades have traditionally been the well-trodden route from the shop floor into management, this is a path that is increasingly likely to become blocked. Not only will there be fewer of these jobs, but those which will exist will almost certainly require such a high technological knowledge that specialist recruitment, probably of graduates, will become the norm. This condemns the ambitious shop floor worker to a working life always at the same state, and this will be a most unpalatable and socially destructive and divisive side effect.

The education system will have to adapt to the new circumstances. The notion of conventional schooling for a life at work is not practicable if a substantial percentage of the pupils will not be able to find work. The lower echelons of the school system in Britain have been described as churning out 'factory fodder', their standards are rudimentary and only the instilling of a routine and discipline comes across. This will have to change as will the types of courses offered. Education will have to spend at least as much time in teaching children about ways of fulfilling themselves, both at work and leisure, as it will in instilling the vocational skills and in the preparation of industrial discipline. The awareness of children is too often unawakened and stimulation not even attempted, so that they have little chance to develop their own personal philosophies. In the future such schooling will not be good enough; it is not merely that we need more teachers, we need a change in educational attitudes. This, however, will only solve part of the problem. School children and schools co-exist, bound together by an unwritten contract. If the children learn to read, write, perform arithmetical tricks and conform they will, at the end of it all, get a job. This has always been the aim of basic schooling. But this contract is increasingly likely to be broken for the jobs will not exist for all.

One argument which crops up again and again when

discussing computer or new technologies is that they are a good thing because they will relieve people of the necessity of doing the dangerous, dirty and boring jobs. Whilst there is some truth in this, it must be recognized that two factors balance it. The first is the deskilling of other jobs and the second is that research in Scandinavia, the U.S.A. and the U.K. suggests that the new types of jobs created are just as unpopular and again described as 'soulless, enervating, boring and repetitive'.

High levels of unemployment have been looked upon in the same way as natural catastrophes; someone must be to blame. Therefore racism, with all its Fascist overtones, is on an upswing. West Indian or Asian immigrants are accused of taking British jobs and so they must be made to go home. Once unemployment starts to rise we get the absurd inconsistency of the racists proclaiming in one breath 'they are taking our jobs' and in the next 'they are living in luxury on the dole'. The truth is that a far higher percentage of black or Asian youths are on the dole than are white youths. The growing militancy of these young people is being inflamed and tapped by fringe ultra-left groups, the only ones who *claim* to care. The response is as negative and destructive as that of the Fascists they are opposing.

The problem clearly becomes worse as unemployment continues to rise. In France there have been disturbances against North African families, in the U.S. racism has not really altered in terms of jobs despite the changes in the legal requirements. Part of the problem in the U.K. is a short-term educational one, which as time passes, should itself pass because, at present, the overall academic standards reached by black children are lower than the average. The solution to this education problem is, of course, a double-edged sword. Once this difference disappears, there will be no excuse at all for any discrepancy in the black/white unemployment ratios within regions. Yet history would suggest that whether this happens or whether the ratio remains the same, racial tension will grow from one side or the other.

Racism is immoral. It is a blind prejudice which appeals to the mass primeval superstitious instincts of mankind, precisely those in fact that society outlaws when they manifest themselves in other ways. The patterns of the 1930s must not be allowed to happen again.

The position as regards women is different. Article after article on discrimination misleadingly starts 'The problems of women and other minority groups ...', but of course women are in the majority. Their problems are different and a special difficulty will undoubtedly arise, especially in Britain. Women have traditionally drifted into and out of the labour force. At one time they worked in the mines and were encouraged to work there, at another when unemployment was high they were encouraged to be good wives and mothers and so it has gone on. In the good times, they stood equal with men as workers, in depressions they were competitive until banished to the kitchen and bedroom. Times, however, have changed, as have attitudes of women.

The Equal Pay Act and the Sex Discrimination Act together have changed the climate regarding the place and role of women in society. Women are joining the labour force more than ever before and demographic projections into the 1980s suggest that this will continue. Schools must now treat boys and girls equally, and as a result more girls may decide to take up careers in jobs and professions previously only thought suitable for boys. Women will expect work, will expect interesting occupations and will expect promotion. The maternity leave provisions should provide the means for this to happen. Yet for all the change in practice and attitude that has occurred, female unemployment has come to stay on a mass basis. Worse than this, future employment will be biased against women.

The types of jobs generally identified with women are the majority of those at risk. Typing (you rarely hear of male typists) and other clerical functions, supermarket employees, bank and insurance staffs, and the indirect production jobs of packing, sorting, and the direct production work of small-scale intricate assembly, are all major candidates for elimination. At the very time women are being encouraged through the educational and legal systems to go to work, the work is collapsing. As a consequence, more girls will have to turn their attentions to the new technologically oriented jobs and thereby compete directly with boys. Quite what will be the result of this is hard to predict. One certainty is that soon we will be sitting through a barrage of articles and TV and radio programmes extolling the virtues and importance of being a good wife and mother again.

Whether this leads to a more militant womens' liberation movement, or signals the end of it as any real force is debatable. But such drastic employment will lead to a traumatic time for women, especially young school-leavers. Interestingly the French Nora Report referred to earlier singles this effect out as a potentially major problem area.

Another obvious problem, mentioned earlier, is the probability that resources will be depleted more rapidly by using the new technologies. Balancing this is the fact that if products get smaller, less materials are needed and less power is required to provide them. In the longer term, however, employment would be threatened by resource depletion itself.

When technology is discussed, with or without its impact on employment, judgements are coloured by the values that people hold. Some believe that science and technology per se are a good thing, and can solve most of the world's outstanding and intractable problems. Scientists must thus be allowed their heads to do what they think fit and it is up to the rest of us to ensure that their discoveries are implemented. Others believe that if technology leads to high growth rates, then that is good because, to them, growth is the key to everything. Others believe that the technology is justified simply because it leads to a greater number and a greater variety of consumer goods. And yet others believe that if the technology gives one country (the speaker's own) an advantage over the others, then the consequent expansion in trade and influence justifies the use of the technology. When employment is added to the discussion these underlying thoughts are bound to influence policies put forward or the remedies available.

Before discussing some of the different remedies that have been advanced, however, one major consideration has to be aired. Any unemployment that arises from technological change will be as a result of a local decision and its effect will be felt locally. It is imperative to realize the importance of this simple fact which was referred to earlier in the book as 'slow death by a thousand cuts'. The person made unemployed in a provincial town does not care whether or not it is in Britain's interests to adopt new technologies overall nor about the macro-economic effects of doing or not doing so for two reasons. The first is that the national economy means nothing real to that person, or indeed to any individual; the second is that any benefits which accrue will not immediately benefit that person. So appeals to the national interest will fall on deaf ears. Even appeals to the longer term interests of families and dependants will find less than an enthusiastic response if that person has to be unemployed and the family suffer in the meantime. There is thus a gap in the perception of the problem. On the one hand individuals see life centred around themselves, on the other, governments see life in the light of a nation as a whole. Where this becomes important is that what is good for the individual often conflicts with what is good for the country. Yet the implementation and introduction of new technologies are necessarily made at the local level, that is at a personal level. It follows that if government believes, as it does, that microprocessor technology is an overall good thing it must approach the issue by assuaging, reassuring and looking after individuals. This should be the major policy aim.

But we must now turn to a consideration of the remedies that have been proposed to the mass unemployment crisis, beginning with the approach which argues that nothing should be done. This is proposed by those, on the one hand, who believe that new mass unemployment will not materialize anyway and, on the other hand, by those who believe that the system itself should be left to sort it out. The former argument cannot be argued except in terms of flatly saying that the premise is wrong. The danger here, of course, is that by the time they have been proved wrong, it will be too late to do anything about the manifestations they alleged would not occur. The second argument, however, is a strange one. It manages to combine an acceptance of the fact that there will be major technical changes leading to unemployment with a touching belief that somehow the system will correct itself and create new jobs. Over the very long term perhaps this might start to become a reality but society could never weather the intervening period. In fact, this form of do-nothing approach is an extremely dangerous one. It allows capitalism full rein and would have to be run at bayonet point. Most people would agree that this is unacceptable, as would be the extreme inequalities in incomes and wealth distribution that would result.

A second solution is to resist the introduction of new

technologies and to carry on as we are today: a latter day Luddism. The first point to make about this is that, referring back to our earlier argument, this is a national strategic response to what will have to be a series of tactical decisions. It is true that the T.U.C. could co-ordinate (not instruct) the trade union movement responses on these lines, but how could any recommendations be enforced? Given the probable size of some of the severance payments (as we have seen in the steel industry) union advice or instructions are likely to be ignored. No doubt there will be some instances where union resistance will be immense and no doubt there will be bitter disputes in some cases. Some of these will undoubtedly be for bargaining purposes, in order to negotiate some sort of acceptable manning levels and job protection guarantees but others will be of fundamental opposition. A union would be remiss in its service to its members if it did not take these attitudes, for after all unions are there to defend the interests of their members primarily in the short term. Employers resist attempts that unions make to get involved in long term decision making, and so most of them in these instances, bear responsibility for the fruits of their intransigence. However, at least two of the areas most at risk, the retail and wholesale trades and the office staffs, have amongst the lowest percentage of unionized sectors in Britain, so there might not be the organization to mount an effective opposition.

Whilst there will be resistance in many areas in the short term, the plan as a long-term strategy will not work. For, if the rest of the world, or even a substantial part of it, adopts the new systems, our products and services will be more expensive, old fashioned, less competitive, and would lose export markets as well as domestic sales. We would also have to isolate ourselves indefinitely from imports as these would be more attractive in terms of price, quality and style than our own production, goods or services. It would seem to be impossible to run a system of import constraints forever given that we have to import so many raw materials and foodstuffs. Another factor, perhaps more minor, would be that trans-national corporations would slowly move out. In the cold wind of world competition and our exposed position, we can put up windbreaks but that is all. The new techniques must be adopted, although if it is any comfort, our competitors, certainly in Europe, will face the same short term troubles.

There is a school of thought, exemplified by Professor Tom Stonier, that the only way out of our troubles is to think small, or smaller, develop alternate technologies to change the pattern of production in Britain, and to expand dramatically the education system. It is an attractive proposition and part of it at least is based on E. F. Schumacher's famous book *Small is Beautiful*. The basic argument is that large corporations are both inefficient and impersonal and no longer can respond to individual needs. Since they will not help in combating unemployment, by devolution much smaller units should be created. The proposal to develop alternate technologies is inevitably part of the small unit argument in that just as it is the large company which uses the capital intensive process, so the freshly defined companies ought to favour the more labour intensive technologies. Such arguments cannot be rejected out of hand, as they have much to commend them, but they do amount to a major switch of attitudes.

Large firms became large principally because they were more efficient. They produced the goods and services which people wanted more cheaply than their competitors, whom they either absorbed or forced out of business altogether. It is true that some businesses became large for less scrupulous reasons or because they controlled the patents (even buying rival ones for suppression), but the primary impulse was that of efficiency. Incidentally, J. K. Galbraith has perceptively stood the argument on its head by theorizing that nowadays big firms only produce what they want people to buy, and given the expenditure on advertising and market research, this is very plausible. A move towards more labour intensive methods implies three consequences: first a slower, more erratic supply of goods; second more expensive goods; third, the unavailability of some goods altogether.

It would take a concerted national decision to opt out of the consumer race and dismantle the large enterprises within the economy. For many reasons we believe that this strategy would founder. In the first place it would take a considerable time, and time is of the essence; at the point at which our present consumer society evolves into anti-consumerism, unemployment would have already been at unacceptable levels for a considerable period. Secondly, it must be granted that this strategy represents a second best solution. We believe that it is possible to achieve a more adequate solution which, whilst improving the quality of life, does not involve material sacrifices. The alternate technology argument postulates that it is mutually inconsistent to have at one and the same time increasing material standards of living and an improving quality of life. It would not be productive to enter into a long discussion of the concept of the quality of life; suffice it to say that it is a very middle class concept which appears to be promulgated by those who have become disillusioned with middle-class ambitions. Our definition of it is quite straightforward; it is to increase people's options. That is why we do not reject this remedy out of hand, it clearly has a role to play.

The official Conservative Party policy to the microprocessor revolution and its effects is, at the time of writing, difficult to define, as by and large they do not appear to have acknowledged the existence of the problem. Two strands of thought seem to appear. The first is that structural unemployment can be defeated by reducing personal taxation and thus increasing incentives. This argument would appear to be self-defeating except in the context of the small labour intensive company run by local businessmen for limited markets. If increasing incentives means to try to make more profits, then these will be made more readily by using the new technologies. If it means to return to risk capital, the same applies; the overall Gross Domestic Product might increase, but only at the expense of a less equitable wealth distribution and higher unemployment. Juxtaposed with further public sector cuts with their subsequent unemployment and the increased overseas investment strategy, it would appear a strange set of policies to increase jobs.

The second string to the argument would appear to be the relaxation of exchange controls, so as to allow extra investment overseas. It is freely admitted that this might be at the expense of domestic manufacturing investment, especially in high technology areas, but it is argued that the returns are high enough that when returned to Britain they would create more wealth. This is the 'rentier economy' solution and really one must ask the simple question – create more wealth for whom? It does, however, get around the technological unemployment problem – no technological advance, only demand deficiency unemployment!

Another proposed solution to the mass unemployment crisis, suggested from quite a different quarter, is to nationalize the main production, distribution and commercial firms. This would either mean that since employment could be controlled and the job criteria used for the firms need not be strictly commercial, employment could be maintained at higher levels than at present for social reasons. Or, more significantly, if all profits accrued directly to the State, the revenue could be applied to either public job creation programmes, or any other public area of need. This would allow the productive firms to use the new technologies to the maximum; indeed it would encourage it as this would lead to greater profits and thus government revenue.

Of necessity there would have to be a very centralized approach, and it has to be admitted that several of the companies would not be viable units; and before the situation changed, unemployment would be too high to sustain the system democratically; the circumstances would force a totalitarian state. Certainly we would not rule out an increase both in public ownership and in public control of industry and commerce, and indeed the whole area of technological change ineluctably points to this as being ultimately the only viable direction in the longer run. And, we do not see a sharp, sudden series of what, in some instances, would have to be expropriations as being the solution to the work problem; indeed we see it as exacerbating the problem quite considerably in the shorter term.

The T.U.C. policy, mentioned at length in the previous chapter, is to cut the working week. Although we disagree with the idea of a 35-hour week as a real help since we believe that a more imaginative, fundamental approach to a working lifetime is needed, the principle is sound. But the T.U.C. policy has been thought through in Britain only as an initial move to tackle the contemporary unemployment situation. If unemployment rises to anywhere near the extent suggested by our argument, it will need more, much more, than a 10 or 10½ per cent reduction in working hours to alleviate the problem. Various studies have been, and are being carried out to quantify the impact on work of such a cut, but in terms of the new technologies, it cannot be more than a one to two relationship at the best. In other words, for every 2 per cent reduction in hours, only 1 per cent more jobs will be saved or created. Thus, a 16 per cent unemployment rate would need a reduction in hours such as to produce a 27·5-hour working week, and the policy would suffer diminishing returns well before this point was reached. The cut in the working week is a weapon, but only one weapon in an armoury, and one that does have to consider the attendant problem of international co-operation and competitiveness.

Another option is the Keynesian one of increasing public spending. This is similar to the second of the nationalization arguments, except that instead of the money accruing directly to the state, it reaches the Exchequer through taxes or levies. Again there is clearly a role for this type of policy but again it suffers from the responses of the trans-national corporations outlined in the previous chapter. In order to fund an unemployment total of 5 million, a public sector borrowing requirement of at least £20 billion (at present prices) would be necessary unless taxation levels were increased. It follows that taxation, almost certainly in the corporate sector, will have to be raised substantially or countries allowed to run with high internal borrowing requirements, or incomes and profits allowed to rise very substantially. As other countries will be facing the same problem, it is highly probable that the international financial community will have to change its attitudes to government expenditure. The only alternative is for it to stick to its guns and buy other guns for client states to use against their citizens!

In Chapter 9, there was a reference to E.E.C. solutions. Amongst European socialists there is a feeling that the time has come for a pan-E.E.C. social contract. This would involve the setting-up of joint ventures in key industries with national ownership or national participation. The Community budget would be totally re-vamped so that only 25 per cent went to agriculture and the rest to social, regional and industrial funds. Again this sort of approach cannot be rejected out of hand, although the E.E.C. dimension is not as necessary in this respect as it is in ensuring co-operation and standardization of approach. On the principle that a trouble shared is a trouble halved, it is sound, but as Chapter 9 noted it does pre-suppose an enormous shift in the political climate of the member states. This is probably a proposal to be stowed away for use in the future if Britain remains a member or more fundamentally, if the E.E.C. itself survives the jobs crisis.

Two other solutions are of possible interest. The first is that work and income should be divorced. If the state paid everyone a decent wage, then work could be done by those who wanted to do it. It could be in co-operatives under local authorities, private entrepreneurs or directly for the state, but in all instances, nearly all, if not all of the profits would accrue to the public purse. This is an ingenious, if ingenuous solution, and we shall come back to one of its ideas in the next chapter. The other proposal was advanced by Colin Hines of Earth Resources. This is that employment could be created and environmental concerns alleviated simultaneously by recycling the materials used in the productively obsolete articles we use to maintain a consumer-based society. This is a viable proposition and one that should be instituted anyway; it would not, however, get anywhere near solving the larger problem of structural unemployment.

What is quite apparent from these and other solutions, from back-to-the-land small-holding based society to labour intensive alternate energy systems, is that although there is something in all of them, there is no one solution. There will have to be a package, and a flexible package at that, if we are to come to terms with this new and vast social problem.

But it is very dangerous to underestimate the strength of those with vested interests which might be damaged or to underestimate the degree of political change required. It is useless to come up with a solution, or a series of them, which are theoretically fine but will not get off the ground. Politically, it would take great courage for a government to impose heavy corporation tax, to encourage public control and to institute proper planning mechanisms. The media in Britain do not take kindly to Labour government proposals, and indeed from all accounts one would believe that we have had rampantly socialist governments in 1964 and 1974 whilst nothing could be further from the truth. Legislation like the Employment Protection

Act, which conferred weak rights on trade unionists and was well behind the standards of Scandinavian and other Northern European legislation was greeted with a tirade of anti-Labour venom. This pettily hostile environment may change but whether quickly enough is open to doubt.

Who in Britain is working on these problems? The Advisory Committee on Applied Research and Development (A.C.A.R.D) set up three sub-committees to enquire into the impacts of new technologies. The first of these on the applications of microprocessors has been published. It is brief and whilst it rightly suggests that Britain must use new technology, it tends to sweep aside any suggestion of consequent large scale unemployment and does not even acknowledge the existence of the word 'processor'. The Central Policy Review Staff is working closely with A.C.A.R.D. but is also producing its own reports. These abound with unsubstantiated assertions that new products will be (not 'may be') developed, that new jobs will be created. The National Economic Development Office has undertaken a study of employment in the 1990s. The Manpower Services Commission is looking at the problem and has commissioned a medium-term economic computer model from Warwick University to help them and the unit for Manpower Studies is now interested.

The Universities of Sussex and Leeds are deeply involved in research, as is Birkbeck College in London and a growing number of private consultancies. On the trade union side, A.S.T.M.S. have produced a lengthy paper which has gone to the T.U.C. and the Labour Party's Home Policy Committee which is looking at the problem. A.P.E.X., I.P.C.S., T.A.S.S. and the E.E.P.T.U. are all interested. The T.U.C. will bring much of this together to report to its 1979 Congress.

Whilst this is all interesting, it is also disturbing. Apart from the Science Policy Research Unit (Sussex University) and selected trade unions' attempt to set up joint research, there has been no co-ordination except on an unofficial level. No government department has yet assumed an overall responsibility nor has yet approached the trade unions – the most intimately affected of all the bodies – for their advice or opinions. The existing inter-departmental discussions are not making good progress. Conferences and seminars proliferate.

Opinion formers meet and form their opinions yet nothing has been done, or looks as though it will be done. Time is starting to run out if we are to prepare for the onslaught and to channel it to everyone's advantage. This, of course, is the real message. The new technologies are not something to be feared. If the right planning, the right political attitudes and the right political decisions prevail, then the world could be a far better place to live in, both for the industrialized and yet-to-be-developed countries. It is far from inevitable that this will happen. A positive and forceful approach is needed to ensure that it does. But it is already too late to do *enough*.

11 A manifesto for change with security

We posed the question at the start of the book 'do people live to work or do they work to live?' At the moment it is clear that the two choices are not looked upon as mutually exclusive. To live, not even well, but just reasonably and moderately in society today people have to work so as to earn the necessary income. Unemployment pay is low, even before the earnings related element stops, and supplementary benefits do not, despite unproven allegations to the contrary, enable the recipients to do anything but exist. These are strictly means tested but now support almost five million people.

At the same time people believe that they *should* work, irrespective of the income problem. Patterns of identity-loss and boredom, vandalism, depression, apathy, and increasingly, anger are the symptoms of unemployment. But we cannot believe that these reactions to loss of work are inherent in human nature. Instead these symptoms represent a series of conditioned responses to the phenomenon, responses which even today are being reinforced by establishment. Each time trade unionists argue publicly for the retention of jobs, work by implication becomes a more desirable commodity, as opposed to being a method of getting income. Yet this attitude will have to change. It can change and in so doing will enable working men, women and their families to enjoy a better life. Work was originally encouraged because without it the goods and services that go to make up the standard of living of people could not have been produced. As much to the point, if not more so, profits would not have been made and capitalism would have been stillborn.

The old methods of production were labour intensive despite all the machinery used and the services that grew up as a result of the real increases in incomes were even more labour intensive. But now these goods and services can be produced using a far lower level of labour and increases in their supply will not produce anything like the corresponding increases in work. The microprocessor allows for a far greater degree of economies of scale than any technology hitherto. From this it would follow that the old notions underlying the work ethic are outmoded. The wheel has turned full circle and it is now in the interests of capitalists to disemploy people if profits are to be made. The only reason why they wish the ethic to remain is to play off one worker against another and maintain a large permanent reserve labour army. If the social costs of this become too great then they will be forced to rethink even this last tenet of faith. As it is employers, by laying-off workers to increase or maintain their profits are in fact passing their costs on to the state. It is the state which has to provide the unemployment and other benefits, not the employer. As income tax and VAT together account for 49 per cent of the total government revenue and these are levied on workers in the main, it is clear that employers are not only shelving their responsibilities but are doing so at the expense of the standard of living of other workers.

Technology makes it easier to provide most of our goods and services. It also makes it cheaper to do so and this can be reflected either in increased profits or cheaper products. But what is it that people want? Do they want more and cheaper goods? Do they want to live longer and in better health? Do they live for and through their children? What sort of goods and services do they want? Are people motivated by a desire to help others or do they have an ingrained capitalist ethic which makes them automatically, inevitably reach for higher incomes or status? Such questions are unanswerable except in vague generalities and yet they are of central importance. Politicians, who have to seek to divine what people want, impose their own value judgements on their answers and run countries accordingly.

The complexities of social class, status and attitudes in a modern industrial state, especially with a long history of reverence for traditions, are daunting. Some people obviously have highly developed senses of social consciousness and justice and demonstrate these in their work or spare time activities. Some have a highly developed sense of acquisitiveness and yet may

159

also be very socially aware. There are no hard and fast dividing lines. Yet all the studies made on working-class life, often paeans of praise by guilt-ridden middle-class graduates, suggest that there is a relative acquiescence in their lot. Ambitions, even for their children, are limited by what they think is practicable given their own and their forebears' experiences. The same sociologists when studying the middle class generally reach the opposite conclusions. The middle class is found to be highly ambitious for success, not only measured in material goods, and definitely so for their children. These points are important. On the one hand people have low expectations (possibly realistic in present circumstances) but a highly developed sense of cohesiveness and collectivity, whilst on the other the opposite obtains, high expectations but an emphasis on individuality. Neither is the wrong way, nor indeed the right way and both are clearly over-simplifications. Both can co-exist and enrich the other, but *not* in an overtly profit oriented society. Neither of the classes actually lives up to its reputation in real life. The working-class culture has been eroded or disrupted by material aspirations and the middle-class quest for individuality has resulted in a version of conformity.

The new technologies, however, can enable society to pursue the goals that it chooses – in other words it opens up options that the system had not previously been able to provide. The options range over those of political systems of communism, socialism or capitalism, through to the very minor ones of choice of products in a brand oriented market. That is why the different motivations are important. It is clear that the choices include room for both of them provided that the development and enhancement of one does not damage the other. In capitalism the growth of the middle class ethic would itself stunt the growth of the collective response, and in centralized socialist states the growth of the collective spirit seems to quarantine individualism. Neither course would serve if consent is to be the main force behind government, for then a middle road for running society will have to prevail. Such a government's policies, though, will have to be different from those which have been practised by governments so far; this is not an argument for 'moderation' as defined by the immobilized forces in our society.

The contemporary situation is intolerable. We have unemployment but can anyone argue that enough goods are being provided, or services given? A substantial portion of the world is starving or near to it, yet in the West obesity and cardiac disease due to overeating is reaching epidemic proportions. The need for health services, including unshown or unshowable demand, is staggering. People die when they should live because resources are scarce; cannot work when they are ill for a reason that could easily have been prevented and are maimed or crippled because of lack of prompt treatment. Yet we have unemployed nurses and doctors emigrating and a mass of unemployed people who could be retrained, because of a system which does not allow this to happen.

We have also built up a complex pyramid of a society. Towns and cities exist, each with their own hierarchies and own social outlets and systems. But for what? Since organized religion collapsed (it pre-dated work by a good 30 years) the motivations for this sort of society have become less clear, although the social systems have become self-perpetuating and a justification in themselves. Whilst this has imparted a high degree of stability, the hierarchies will not be able to withstand the pressures arising out of the third industrial revolution. The present structures were formed as a result of the first industrial revolution and amended by the second. It seems clear that with all options open further amendment will occur and a new set of targets and justifications will emerge.

This is but one area where, as the world alters, so attitudes have to change too. The attitudes to mobility and travel changed first with the steam engine and then the motor car and, in so doing, many protective walls erected around shaky institutions fell. Village life and squirearchies could not survive comparison with the towns. The public bar has all but disappeared from pubs, the phone-in programmes are dominated by people who, only 2 years ago, would have been frightened to be on the radio. History is in fact a record of these alterations and as society changes more quickly so a time-lag is manifested in the responses to the change. Social responses have always been slow in Britain but ultimately pressures bring an upheaval of some sort if the changes do not take place within a reasonable time. The changes in attitude are very marked in a social sense.

Approaches to marriage, divorce, pre-marital relationships, abortion and homosexuality have all changed over a relatively short space of time, often overturning the major props and taboos of society in the process.

Politicians and politics and government have been part of this change too. In 1910 it was unthinkable that women should vote in Britain and further back in the mid-nineteenth century when the Tory M.P., Mr Giddy, got up in the House to oppose a limited education bill and said 'Better a brutal starving nation than men with thoughts above their station', he was adumbrating a substantial political viewpoint. Since then the Welfare State, the Health Service and the government's intervention into all forms of industry, commerce and life have occurred, unthinkable intrusions only four decades ago. Each reformist or interventionist measure has been greeted with prophesies of the collapse of the nation, or at least its moral fibre, and this reaction will undoubtedly occur again and again.

Large-scale unemployment, especially amongst the young, is a fertile ground for political agitation and reaction: extremist policies of the right and left have the attraction of radicalism and advantage that as the policies are unlikely to be implemented there is no need to be constrained by responsibility or practicability. It is starting to happen now, with our *present* unemployment rates. Yet we must remember that history shows that Monday's extremism is often Wednesday's conventionalism and Friday's conservatism, and not dismiss the more worthwhile and sensibly based movements out of hand. Those movements which history has time and again cast into the dustbin, Fascism included, must be opposed, but those with the constructive proposals, even if *presented* negatively, deserve attention.

Conventional politics itself will have to change too. One particular facet is in political propaganda. It is thoroughly dishonest of the Tory Party to advertise, using 'dole queues' as a peg and pretending that they have an answer when they have not even broached the subject. Politicians will have to learn, and quickly, to trust the public and tell them the truth, as must trade unions with their members and employers with their employees. There is already an unhealthy mistrust by the public of politicians and the present avoidance of the true workless future will intensify this if the public are not told that unemployment is unlikely to fall. The consequences of such a growth in corrosive disbelief could be devastating for democracy. This book and this chapter in particular, is dedicated to the proposition that democracy is the most desirable form of government, but democracy requires that information be provided to the electorate so that it may make a rational choice at election time; if this is withheld wilfully then we have a sham. In addition people sharply react on perceiving they have been fooled and when they discover the truth they tend to round on the culprit with anger. Open government is more than a slogan, it is a democratic essential.

Politicians then must change both policies and attitudes but their changes will be dwarfed by the changes that will take place in people's attitudes to work. People will have to realize that full-time work itself only has the value that they themselves put on it when actually at the work place and this is often a negative one. That people will 'have to' is a deliberately strong construction because circumstances will be such that if they do not, the resulting social upheavals will probably prevent anyone from working regularly. If we assume that people want consumer goods, personal services as well as state social services, then a system will have to be found to provide them for all, even if they are not working at all or only part of the time. If this were to be done then we believe that the attitudes to work would swiftly change. It can be done, indeed must be done. The expectation of a life at work – the present one for school-leavers – should be changed to life, with leisure and work taking equal priorities. In truth, the prospect of a full lifetime working is a depressing one given the unpleasantness of most jobs and actual dislike of some of them. Horizons and ambitions must be, and should be, lifted above this very low threshold.

The concept of job security should be changed to *'whole life security'*. Whether in or out of work people should be wanted and secure, their families not discouraged, and the unemployed themselves not made to feel inadequate.

We only get a significant block of leisure on retirement, and then we are too old to enjoy many of the facilities that are available for the younger elements of society. This is surely absurd. What it means is that we are working to continue working, not to enjoy the fruits of the work-money and what it

163

can buy. Not all leisure activities have a price, however, and we deprive ourselves even of these by our insistence on working from 16 or 18 or 21 up to 60 or 65 in one continuous, hard stretch. No wonder so many people die just before or after retirement; after all that work there is even less chance for available time in which to enjoy leisure. Leisure is not only rest or hedonistic enjoyment. Leisure activities can be constructive and rewarding for both the person and society in general, and whether this is in the nature of gardening or undertaking voluntary work amongst the old or handicapped young or even making one's expertise available to another set of people, the principle remains the same. But this cannot be undertaken in an insecure situation, which means that the concept of whole life security must become the paramount objective, for only then can we mix adequately leisure and work.

The current objective of a 35-hour week is both too limited in its effect on unemployment and too modest in its approach to the welfare of workers. It reflects traditional attitudes at a time of changing circumstances, and as such simply is inadequate. It is recognized that many members of trade unions already work less than a 35-hour-week: some clerical staffs work $33\frac{1}{2}$ hours, the 9-day fortnight is commonplace already, and in any case certain production processes militate against such a policy anyway. But a cut of 1 hour off each working day will merely mean that a person will have to cope with the rush hour on all 5 days, get up early on all 5 days and suffer all the daily disadvantages of working whilst not having any significant period of time in which to develop other activities.

The fact that many processes will require a four-shift system as a result of this change makes matters even worse. The British social system still does not cope with shift work. The hours of pub opening, shop and restaurant availability and leisure activity potential are virtually restricted to those people whose lives revolve around day shift working. This is not an international phenomenon. In France, Germany, Italy or the U.S.A. the availability of these services means that complex shift working carries with it fewer disadvantages. Thus, any changes to working and overtime hours on an E.E.C. level which would mean an extension of the 'Continental shift system' would be welcomed less warmly in the U.K. than elsewhere. Recent U.S.

research has shown that stress conditions related to less sleep, unsatisfactory home life and an upsetting of diurnal rhythms are more prevalent in shift than non-shift workers. It would seem foolish to produce a policy with such side-effects when other remedies are available.

The whole approach to working time must be treated on a working lifetime basis. To start with, a prime objective must be to reduce the number of weekly or monthly trips to work. A 4-day week, on an 8-hour day basis is more likely to require the taking on of more extra workers than a reduction of 1 hour per day, which can be covered more easily with shift and pattern changes. In addition, it would enable workers to cope with leisure in that a large amount of time, on a regular basis, would be released and, given that leisure activities often involve travel, the time factor is important. If our projections of unemployment are correct and this method of job sharing is adopted then by the year 2000 the working week will have to become a three times 8-hour day.

However, there are structural imbalances which reduce the usefulness of such measures as job creators or savers. To start with, more women than men will become disemployed; secondly, the ability of an enterprise to sustain more employment may be in question. Regional imbalances in industry, employment, skills, sex and race all go to make this an imperfect proposition.

Nevertheless, we believe that it should be adopted. Partly because of its consequences for employment, small in relation to the problem though they may be, but mainly because workers deserve it – *it is a natural collective bargaining development* to obtain better terms and conditions of employment. However, this is not all that should be looked at and changed if necessary. For example, why not work 3 weeks per month or have an extra month's holiday each year? Then there is the question of sabbaticals. University teachers, Fleet Street journalists, some senior managers (and U.S. blue-collar steelworkers) have had these for many years; why not extend the principle to all workers? If workers had just 1 year off in a lifetime this would only add – at most – $2\frac{1}{2}$ per cent to salary bills so that at least four such Sabbaticals in a working lifetime (one every 10 years), are feasible. Different systems could apply to different types of work and production or commercial methods. These types of changes in combination would have the advantage of providing regular blocks of leisure with longer stretches, at planned intervals. Such a combination would give average family members the chance to plan their lives together rather than living them on a work-related and *ad hoc* basis. In addition retirement ages should be flexible but the same for both men and women. Some people in some jobs, miners, for example, wish to retire early, others do not. It would be perverse in the extreme to impose early retirement and thus lose a wealth of experience and expertise *unless* methods are found to make these attributes available to others on perhaps a teaching or consultancy basis within formal retirement.

This system which, as we have repeatedly said, will have to be adopted internationally, would obviously imply both a decreased labour productivity and decreased profits. However the multiplier effects of more people at work should guarantee some other market expansions. Employers would appear to have little option in the matter: they can either settle for lower profits or resist the changes. If they resist then governments will have to provide far higher levels of unemployment pay and other social payments and the revenue would have to come from corporate profits, taxation or measures of nationalization. As we have argued, expectations of material good are now far too high for any other options to be adopted on a basis of consent. If employers become totally intransigent the result could be a totalitarian society which imposes the high unemployment levels by force. We do not believe that the British people would allow this to happen.

Two reflections relate to this argument. The first is that by using the new technologies no further employment may be needed even if the lifetime work package is adopted. In Britain today there is very low productivity and a high level of over-manning. A forced taking-on of labour has the same effect as a negative payroll tax, or a change of control, or both, and also implies unnecessarily expensive goods and services. Would it not be better gradually to train people not to go to work just for the sake of it but to work in vital areas of demand and need? We believe that to work as an act of devotion to the concept of working, especially if it results in a loss to the general welfare is an absurd concept. Even so there will, no doubt, be *some* take-up of labour, however limited, but the whole exercise must be preceded by international agreement. The British government should be talking now on a bilateral and multilateral basis to other governments and putting the case for change. At the same time the E.E.C. must start to work on the problem amongst its member states. Trade unions must co-ordinate their claims and their actions, both in national strategy terms and in terms of common claims affecting the working life of employees of trans-national company groups in each of their countries. In these respects governments and unions should work together where their political philosophies make this practicable. The government itself should start to show an example by implementing these decisions where it is the direct employer, although we believe that considerable re-deployment can and should take place in many of the governmental sectors.

The shorter working lifetime, coupled with the expansion of leisure, can be made possible by the released resources from the new technologies. They can, over the long term, reduce some of the resulting unemployment problems but in any event there will still be a considerable number of people unemployed. Unemployment pay must therefore be paid at around the national average wage. There must be no financial penalty attached to being workless. It will be the systems, not the workers themselves which would be responsible and thus it would be immoral to retain the present financial penalties; those unemployed will be sacrificed for greater benefits for others and in the twentieth century sacrifices are frowned upon. In economic terms this is desirable too. The extra income being circulated by virtue of the increased consumption would enable national economies to continue to expand and maintain a reasonable level of goods and services. If the prices system does not alter, given the new technical systems, then profits will be far higher, and if prices either fall or rise less than incomes then the extra real disposable income can be used for the purchase of more goods and services, which in turn generate more profits. Either way the reserve will be there. In social terms it is obviously desirable for the unemployed, especially the young, not to feel economically deprived because they cannot find a job, and it would almost certainly be a stabilizing factor in a potentially unstable situation. It is sometimes difficult or impossible to attribute responsibility exactly for people who have been made redundant as technological employment can be at one or two stages removed from the particular job. For example a TV manufacturer could have slumping sales because of a technological development in an overseas competitor's product and as a result domestic tastes change. The alternative is so to widen the definition as to encompass the example above; this then becomes so all-embracing that an overall high payment would cost little more. Whichever definition is used there will always be the marginal cases on the wrong side of the line; these should be avoided. A new high unemployment payment will be the basis upon which total life security will depend. Security is much sought after and as the new technologies will have the critical side-effect of reducing it, the need for positive and corrective action is central.

Britain and other industrialized countries have not yet managed to satisfy all the desires and all the needs of their populations. In relation to consumer goods there are still substantial minorities who either have not enough to eat or are inadequately clothed and housed. Some have no radio, TV set, car, telephone, or little furniture so there is a potential demand for these and many other products, allowing for the fact that some people actually do not want them. Given that a better income distribution and increases in unemployment pay can go some way to meeting this criterion, as can the workers taking a share of the increased productivity, then a stimulus to general demand will result. This could result in a marginal increase in available work, but as we have suggested earlier, no more than this. In addition the increased reliability or higher efficiency may make some people replace existing products earlier than they would otherwise have done, but this will be a once and for all windfall gain.

But there are other needs. Health, education, social welfare, the elderly, public transport, museums, exhibitions and entertainment are all in short supply or not matching demand. There is an enormous need for such services and in the health-care field alone there is literally an infinite requirement. Social welfare, be it remedial, pre-emptive or monitoring, is obviously a labour intensive area as is education, with both of them depending on one-to-one relationships. Both education and the health services are capable of being improved by the use of new technologies, but as an adjunct to employees, not, in most instances replacing them. In Britain both services are primarily provided by the state and both obviously could be improved. An explosion in employment is possible in all of these people-oriented service industries. Pre-emptive medicine using a system of regular check-ups would ultimately reduce costs and also ensure greater security, happiness and health to people. In such a labour intensive industry more doctors, dentists, ancillary workers and professionals could be trained and positive programmes established. The education system needed to cope with this process will have to be radically expanded and reformed. Again, this is in itself labour intensive and could absorb a considerable amount of the unemployment created in other areas.

Education needs to be adapted in many ways. We have already suggested that a wider approach shall be adopted both to enable people to fulfil their own potential and to expand their options for leisure activity. Technologists and scientists must be trained not only for application to conventional work levels but also generally up to post-doctoral standards; electronics must become one of the major disciplines. Inter-disciplinary teaching needs to be used more especially with electronics as an option. There should be a huge expansion of in-house or industrial training to cope with the short term re-orientation that will be needed as a result of the new technologies and also to cope with the retraining consequent upon other secondary changes. These come about because of the ever increasing rate of technological change. The initial development will merely claim paternity for the family of ensuing developments so that it may well be that a person will need considerable retraining three or four times in a working lifetime, if there are tasks to be retrained for. Finally and crucially provision is required for life-long education. People should be enabled, if they wish, to use education and knowledge as an end in itself, to treat it as a leisure activity and at all levels. The unemployed should have priority in access to all educational establishments; they should be free to make major changes in their careers at least twice in a lifetime and to be provided with the necessary resources.

A programme to provide housing, available on a more flexible pattern and encouraging mobility, should be established as again this is a labour intensive activity and could soak up some unemployment after suitable training or re-training. The British housing stock is poor and old, especially in the city centres, and its rehabilitation should be a priority along with the abolition of involuntary overcrowding and homelessness. A hard look must be taken at housing policy. Local authority housing clearly acts as a bar to mobility in that whilst waiting-lists exist people who move have to go to the bottom of the queue in the area to which they have transferred. One satisfactory approach might be some form of Housing Association expansion, but with public accountability and safeguards. This is a vital factor, for if unemployment is to be minimized and services provided, geographical mobility is a basic prerequisite.

We have mentioned the issue of staffing in local and central government and the likelihood that the new technologies will not affect this. But there are services in these sectors that are chronically understaffed or which do not even exist although there is an evident need for them. Most of these services will provide direct public contact jobs as the tasks of informing and explaining policies to people, monitoring and following up social work and other service provisions and case study work tend to go by the board as the administration departments increase in size at present. We believe that retraining people to do these sorts of jobs would be beneficial both for the employee and society, but especially for those who cannot cope over-well with the complex exigencies of a modern industrial state. It would certainly improve the benefit/cost ratio of rates and taxes. Improvements are needed in public transport, especially in the large urban and sparsely populated rural areas where such transport is now skeletal.

These public sector service provisions could provide the partial answers to two distinct problems simultaneously. The overall quality of life, especially for those in the greatest need, could be improved whilst employment can be created. It is, however, idle to pretend that such a programme could be initiated and financed in sufficient time to cope with increasing unemployment. The political, training, retraining, and sheer logistical problems are immense, as are the social adjustment consequences for individuals.

Large businesses, like governments, have developed bureaucracies of their own and can be as rigid, inflexible and authoritarian. They are also likely to become even more capital intensive. People in Britain like to have human contact, especially in the service sector such as shops or banks, and there is also a small, but growing demand for hand-made craft goods of all descriptions. As small businesses tend to be more labour intensive than the larger ones they should be encouraged. Yet there are limits to the growth in this sector. For one of the factors of the new technology is that it is making automation possible for small batch production, or small office facilities, because its price is so low relative to labour costs; indeed, some microcomputers are being advertised in the national press with just this point as the main attraction. Equally the cost and service differentials will always ensure a limited market for hand-made goods.

There is a school of thought which asserts that the larger corporations will voluntarily give up some of their functions and actually encourage small businesses to take them over. They would have an equity, but non-controlling stake and act as technological and managerial consultants. If this sounds altruistic the motives are not just those of public relations purposes but for the sound commercial reasons that such actions will aid profit maximization – not to be confused with revenue maximization. Such a system would act as a boost to small enterprises. It is also certainly worth considering a large expansion of the co-operative system using either the National Co-operative Development Agency or local authorities as the provider of initial and working capital. It would be, however, both unrealistic and wasteful to create co-operatives or other small businesses to produce goods or services for which there is no demand. But there is clearly a role for this sort of enterprise in creating some employment, in providing specialized and personalized goods and services and also in encouraging the crafts, skills and the arts generally.

One clear growth area of employment will be leisure industries themselves. These encompass a whole range of products and services such as hotels, restaurants and cafes, gardening equipment and products; gardeners, actors, radio and TV workers, sports and sportsmen, artists and all the equipment used in these activities are just part of these industries. Clearly the radio, hi-fi and videotape manufacturing industries will become more capital intensive but others are labour intensive. The growth in leisure will follow naturally from the change in emphasis in the educational system and the extra leisure time from those at work plus those who are unemployed.

Both the arts and the theatre should receive a tremendous stimulus and imaginatively one could envisage a new twentieth century age of creativity. Many people argue that creativity is an instinctive urge in mankind and that the de-skilling of jobs – and certainly the increased automated repetition – is responsible for industrial alienation. If this is so then the pent-up expression of people might be allowed full rein.

The aim in our proposals is to change the balance in society. The overwhelming majority – or those who work or need to work – will for the first time be the prime recipients of the returns of the means of production rather than the returns going to those who originally provided the capital. This is a simplistic view in that the growth of compulsory contributions to pension funds and insurance offices has progressed to such an extent that, collectively, the work force is on its way theoretically to having a controlling interest in most domestic stock exchange quoted companies, although at present not a functional control. Even the most dedicated Marxists are now shareholders at one remove. But the change is nevertheless real for all that. It requires authors and playwrights, artists and actors, musicians and clowns all to make the working and middle classes believe in themselves and to believe in their right to the better things in life; the horizons must first be identified, then aimed for.

Finally there is the question of being able to control our own destinies. For centuries the various systems have moulded people into the shapes which were best for the systems; individuals used to be powerless to influence the process. Most people had little choice from the accident of which social strata they were born into and what educational system instructed them. The new technological revolution allows us to get nearer breaking this mould, in the first place by providing the means of doing so through the information and communication technology available and secondly by enabling the structure of work and society to change.

Our broad policies will involve not only the maintenance of political democracy but also the introduction of industrial democracy. Employees will have to, and inevitably must, get involved in the strategic decision making of their employers and probably on a trans-national basis. This must not be a semblance of power without authority, nor can it be, as an American trade unionist put it, 'a minority stake in success but a majority stake in failure'. We have argued that any democratic authority will have to revise its attitude to the control of corporations and that a drift to public ownership and/or control (and certainly accountability) is inevitable. This inevitability is because the inter-relationships between companies, and between companies and governments, are so dense and complex as to make planning of the use of resources impossible without these changes. And planning will, as we have demonstrated, be needed to avoid all the totalitarian traps along the road. Planning and collectivism both have unfortunate connotations in Britain; somehow they suggest manipulation and subservience, and are associated with austerity, repression, uniformity and conformity.

The sorts of planning and collective responses that we are talking about are far removed from these misleading definitions. We need to regain the freedoms that the modern industrial state has removed and to do so we must act collectively. In fact, the collective society has already arrived and, in Britain at least, individuals do not seem to have suffered. But still we do not plan, we cobble together packages in response to situations. This planning must involve employees at all levels and it must ensure that goods and services are produced either with an eye to exporting or substituting for imports and to meet demands and needs. It must bring in the social dimension, taking as its main theme the welfare of the majority.

There needs to be a revolution in attitudes to match the third industrial revolution. This must primarily be in relation to work and leisure. We need to guarantee security; we need international action and co-operation; we need to re-establish control over our lives and we need to plan our responses to the future. We believe that these are the minimum basic points that emerge from the collapse of work.

173

12 *Prevention is better than cure*

It is a time for action, not words; a time for policy implementation, not electoral promises. The action must cover two separate things: preparations for the ever-increasing unemployment levels and the setting-up of mechanisms to ensure that the collapse of work is transmuted into a policy of leisure.

First we must ensure that we do indeed get our technological revolution and that we get it early enough. It is obvious that industrialists have been loth to invest in Britain for many years and, as we have explained, this has much to do with our present parlous economic and competitive position. We have also argued that the British system itself militates against investment in high technology or high risk areas. Whilst certain companies will undoubtedly make the transition quickly enough, others will not and will somehow have to be made to do so. The actual involvement in, and development of micro-processor technology is the case in point; it took the state-funded National Enterprise Board to seize the opportunity. The similarly financed National Research Development Corporation has also been active in this field.

In this sense it is fortunate that the Government, and Prime Minister James Callaghan in particular, has taken a positive stance, and is obviously aware of the benefits of the micro-electronic revolution, although regrettably declines to acknowledge the possibility of a negative side. However, Government money is being made available to the amount of £400 million at 1978 prices. The money is to be spent in three main areas. To establish a high volume production capacity for silicon chips through the N.E.B/INMOS project. To provide capability for micro-electronics products for user companies, and thirdly to increase industry's awareness of the potential and availability of the new technologies. In conjunction with this employment training projects are being developed, one of which will train an additional 3000 people in software skills by late 1979, whilst also acting on the basic education system and its curriculum. Finally, and very importantly, the Government plans to use public sector purchasing as a lead to encourage the application of micro-electronics wherever possible. But this plan is deficient in two respects. It does not face up to unemployment problems, instead it relies on the C.P.R.S.'s generalized optimism; more crucially it does not face up to the British lack of investment problem.

We are fortunate in that the arrival of the new technologies has coincided with the development of North Sea oil and gas resources. We are unfortunate in that their arrival also coincides with the increase in the potential labour force and the employment emancipation of women. However, from the point of view of investment in new capital, in design and in research the North Sea oil revenues will be invaluable.

Two new public sector funds need to be created immediately. The first would be based on North Sea revenues. This could fund a new government agency to the tune of £100,000,000 per year. The agency would be a government-backed research and development, design and marketing facility which, initially at least, would concentrate on process development using micro-electronics. It would act on a client basis, hold patents in its own name and sell the licences to companies. It is not an original proposal for we would just be reversing the traditional roles and be copying the Japanese principle. Such an agency could and should be self-financing over time. It should also act with existing agencies such as the National Enterprise Board and the National Research Development Corporation to set up wholly owned or partly owned enterprises, in the high technology areas. It would also liaise with bodies such as the Science Research Council and government departments, and research institutes such as the Medical Research Council. The lack of an effective industrial infrastructure of this nature is one of the major reasons behind our long decline, and a crash programme is desperately needed.

The rest of the North Sea funds, perhaps another £2 billion

175

per year, should be applied to the National Enterprise Board, the Scottish and Welsh Development Agencies and the Co-operative Development Agency for direct investment purposes.

The second fund to be set up would involve the pension funds. These are now the biggest single institutional investors in Britain, handling 26 per cent of all personal savings. As we have argued, by and large the pension funds do not actually invest in productive industry, not only because of their own structures, but also because of the Stock Exchange. The fund could take roughly £1 billion per year out of the new income of the pension industry and invest it in British industry, probably in smaller companies. It could be administered on a tripartite basis, government, industry/city and trade unions. Members of the pension funds would not be at risk as the government would underwrite or reinsure the 'loan' at a rate of return commensurate with actuarial calculations of the liabilities of funds. One might even create a 'pension industrial gilt'. This sort of fund has been proposed by the T.U.C. in its evidence to the Committee to Review the Functioning of Financial Institutions chaired by Sir Harold Wilson.

Contradictory though it may seem, we accept that in ensuring that Britain modernizes its industrial capacity and regenerates itself, we are in fact also guaranteeing rising unemployment. However, as we have pointed out, it is either unemployment for this reason or unemployment due to a low growth, lack of investment environment. Although the projected unemployment rates are similar, there is a vital qualitative difference. Technological unemployment will be based on high growth, high profits and returns, a highly competitive manufacturing and service base and high incomes, and these enable constructive policies to be adequately funded. The low growth unemployment, on the other hand, is accompanied by low profits, low productivity, low incomes and is a desperate if not terminal situation.

The next practical step is to ensure that these new technologies are embraced by trade unionists. We have already explained why they should accept them and why the trade union movement would give them their support. However, various pre-conditions will have to be met if obstructive tactics are not to be encountered. It cannot be too strongly emphasized that these measures must be adopted and the mechanisms set up *before* the major redundancies start. In practice that means they should be introduced starting within the next two years.

Unemployment pay must be increased dramatically, high severance or redundancy pay negotiated, and for school attendance or early pensions, for example, increased or introduced since it is clear that many of those made redundant, especially those over 50 years old, will never work again. Employers will have to recognize that if the redundancies aid their profits then those who, by their going, helped to create this situation should share in those profits on a continuing basis. These could be in the form of lump sums or continuing wage payments on top of redundancy and unemployment benefits.

Education and retraining schemes will have to be in operation *before* the redundancies take place. The education budget should be immediately expanded, oriented towards adult education, and to this end more teachers should be trained – starting now. If new buildings are necessary, or modifications to existing buildings, then work on them should also begin at once. In addition to this, technical colleges, polytechnics and universities should start courses in micro-electronics and systems analysis and start to produce a sizeable number of young people capable of using, designing and teaching the new technologies.

Unions will have to defend their members by getting the best possible redundancy terms and also arranging for the most painless method of leaving. This is generally accepted as being a combination of a no-involuntary-redundancy agreement, early retirements, and voluntary redundancy; in other words by 'natural wastage'. However, if unions are successful in this it will inevitably mean that a high proportion of the unemployment will be amongst the young as enterprises will no longer be taking on much new labour. School-leavers by definition, have never worked, they have never been members of trade unions and are thus unrepresented. They have no political voice, no pressure points and are thus vulnerable to the blandishments of political fringe groups, especially as they had been led to believe that jobs were available.

This in itself is de-stabilizing. It is clear that forms of

representation must be hammered out and it is also clear that trade unions must liaise with these representatives at factory, district, regional and national levels. This course of action must be followed by similar Government and employer initiatives. The young have every right to have high expectations and even higher ideals and neither should be stifled at birth. On a practical short term basis continuing education must be encouraged using, amongst other things, a school attenders' grant, payable to all students over 16 years old.

Money should be made available to those being made redundant to set up either small businesses or co-operatives if they can satisfy local development boards that there is a demand for the goods or services which they aim to produce; the second of our two funds could be used for this purpose. Local authorities should be compelled either to give rate concessions or rent council-owned factory or other industrially zoned accommodation over substantial periods. In connection with this the Lucas Aerospace workers have demonstrated that a workforce is perfectly competent to produce viable plans of its own. This initiative, unsuccessful though it has been in practical terms may well prove to be a turning point in the achievement of industrial self-confidence and awareness among the workforce. It certainly denies the notion that employees are non-thinking people who do not want to know about either the future of their employers or are uninterested in the products they produce.

The statutory notice of impending redundancies will have to be increased from its 30 to 90 day period to a 6 month minimum. Again this change must be instituted quickly. Without these minimum requirements, which together only start to give financial security and hope for the future for unemployed people, there will be major opposition to changes in work techniques, in microprocessor introduction and against any redundancies.

Whilst these minimum preconditions will assist in preparing the way for the acceptance of the new technologies, there is no guarantee that they will be successful. The troubles in Fleet Street, and at *The Times* newspaper especially, with the introduction of technological change demonstrate this quite clearly. The technology in question there was not this new wave, but in essence an old and tried one. What is also true is that they will make substantial contributions if only because they demonstrate quite clearly that elements other than technology are changing and that the movement towards the serious treatment of serious unemployment has started.

Trade unions must also move quickly in the short term. Their international links should be strengthened and more resources devoted to them so that co-ordination of actions and claims can be achieved across national frontiers. Additionally British unions must welcome and train trade unionists from the L.D.C.s so that they may be able to defend their members' interests in a more organized way when the new industrial processes reach them.

The movement to industrial democracy must accelerate. It must not be allowed to become a subject which gives employment only to H.M.S.O. staff as they print and sell successive Reports, White and Green Papers. If the changes in work methods and prospects are to be embraced by those workers and employees who will have to operate them, then they must have a say in decision making before implementation, indeed, before the plans are drawn up. The new technologies will add a new dimension to industrial democracy as well as increase the urgency of its implementation. Along with any government action in this field the idea of Planning Agreements has to be revised, adapted and implemented both from the point of view of trade unions and of planning in general terms. The Chrysler débâcle has shown that the original concept was deficient; in future such agreements will have to be legally binding and compulsory.

Although planning agreements would cover the generality of future working conditions, and technological changes in industrial democracy extension also help, there is a need for specific knowledge and action. In this respect we would like to see the negotiating of Norwegian-style technological agreements and the appointment of technology shop stewards and representatives. The Association of Cinematograph Television and Allied Technicians has already negotiated an implementation of technology agreement with the Independent Television Authority. The traditional employers' response to this form of request or negotiation is that commercial secrecy must prevail. This is simply not good enough in these new circumstances – it

179

can be accomplished in Norway without commercial damage taking place, so it can happen here.

There are other short term actions which need to be taken quickly. Britain should take the initiative in bringing about international action. The government should raise the matter at the Council of Ministers of the E.E.C. and insist on action – and keep insisting. Britain should open discussions with the United States, with Japan, and with other industrialized countries on a bilateral basis to explore the possibility of international concordats. Britain should raise this matter at U.N.C.S.T.D. and world agencies dealing with developing countries and within the framework of the Commonwealth Institute and Conference. All these meetings have to be set up as a matter of some urgency given the time it takes actually to reach international agreements. Finally, these questions will also have to be raised with the Comecon countries and China.

A separate Planning Commission should be established. It would liaise with N.E.D.O. and its sector working parties and N.E.D.C.s and it would ultimately have the responsibility of producing strategic plans. It could co-ordinate the efforts of government departments and agencies, such as the Manpower Services Commission and the Training Services Agency, and it should base its information on planning agreements. Once again this is not a new concept. Both France, and Sweden (with its Labour Market Board) have operated this system successfully for years. It is not, however, desirable to have all planning and decisions made at central levels. Local planning agencies should be set up with a considerable degree of autonomy and these would be able to tap into the two new funds which we recommend at the outset. These proposals are again needed in the short term.

Further, public sector expenditure should be expanded over and above the educational system's urgent requirements. The training of medical personnel should be a priority as should a capital expenditure expansion in new hospital building and equipment purchase. In other areas where need exists and hardship is manifest the services should be expanded so as to cope. But whilst it would be easier to try to eliminate existing unemployment levels by expanding the public sector we feel that it would be a short-sighted approach. Government revenues are urgently required for the other matters and these have a greater long-term impact. To expand the totality of public sector services now would be to make their future even more uncertain in that we must have a burgeoning industrial and manufacturing base *before* we can guarantee the revenues for all the services we need. In other words create the wealth at the same time as re-distributing the wealth and in a way that it can be re-distributed.

The new technologies make one thing apparent. Industry and commerce cannot be left to make and implement short-term decisions on output and manpower on their own; to do so would be to invite social disaster. Their motives would lead to haphazard growth and unforeseen redundancies, both of which are undesirable in any circumstances. The market's allocation of resources thus cannot be left alone and intervention is the only long-term answer. The political conflict is sharpened by the new technologies – the need for planning becomes the essential part of the political debate, rather than an optional extra. In addition, to fund the high levels of unemployment, to provide the public services and the consequent employment or to have changed working circumstances over a life-time will require exchequer monies. This is clearly a political decision and a fundamental one. The alternative is to create a very unstable society only capable of being run with the naked use of force. Our suggested changes would be logical and rational and ultimately lead to a socialist, humanitarian and gratifying society.

In the course of this book we have covered the national terrain of new and old data which in total has received scant attention from politicians, from academics, from businessmen or from trade unions. Despite the fact that these technologies have existed for 15 years and despite the fact that they have been used industrially for the past 5 years it is only within the past year that any serious public thought has been given to the implications of their introduction within Britain. This is partly a function of our government system. A five year span is not an encouragement to long-term strategic planning. But it is also partly because we have so few qualified scientists and engineers in positions of business or political responsibility. And it is also partly because overall our academic system remains firmly rooted in traditional disciplines and the analysis of our new problems requires an inter-disciplinary approach.

It is impossible to over-dramatize the forthcoming crisis as it potentially strikes a blow at the very core of industrialized societies – the work ethic. We have based our social structures on this ethic and now it would appear that it is to become redundant along with millions of other people. To accommodate this shock there will have to be major changes throughout society. Recent past experiences do not help. Neither the recent technological changes nor the unemployment were similar. We shall find ourselves in a position diametrically opposed to the one we are in today. Now we have inflation, a slump and rising unemployment. In 15 or 20 years time we shall have a boom, minimal inflation, high growth and the largest unemployment in our history. We will not be alone – so will many other industrialized countries.

It is not a prospect at which we should quail or rush to the nearest bunker. This is an opportunity to rethink our traditional attitudes and to accept boldly the new opportunities. It is an occasion for hope, not despair, and those who are panicking or suggesting it might not happen must pause. Societies have never evolved as smoothly and inevitably as historians and hindsight would sometimes suggest. The great leaps forward have in the past been preceded by bloody adventures, famines, plagues or wars. Perhaps we are lucky. Our next leap forward is preceded by a small 1 or 2 mm square thin object and it may be the measure of the civilization of mankind that this can change our social, political and industrial lives where before it took far more terrible circumstances and events.

The jobs holocaust can be moderated but only if we have a multi-dimensional approach now.